William Reiser, S.J.

Forever Faithful:
The Unfolding of
God's Promise to Creation

D1557051

A Michael Glazier Book
THE LITURGICAL PRESS
Collegeville, Minnesota

A Michael Glazier Book published by The Liturgical Press

Cover design by Greg Becker

Imprimi potest: Very Rev. William A. Barry, S.J.
                Provincial, Society of Jesus of New England

1   2   3   4   5   6   7   8   9

Library of Congress Cataloging-in-Publication Data

Reiser, William.
    Forever faithful : the unfolding of God's promise to creation /
William Reiser.
        p.   cm.
    "A Michael Glazier book."
    ISBN 0-8146-5849-0
    1. God—Promises. 2. Creation. 3. Jesus Christ—Resurrection.
4. Church. 5. Holy Spirit. 6. God—Love. 7. God—Worship and love.
I. Title.
BT180.P7R45   1993
231.7—dc20   93-15191
                                                            CIP

For the Members of the Catholic Alumni Sodality
of Our Lady of Worcester County

"Your promise gives me life."

(Psalm 119:50)

Contents

Introduction 1

Chapter One
Creation as Promise 19

Chapter Two
Resurrection as Promise 42

Chapter Three
The Church as Sign of God's Promise 57

Chapter Four
Spirit as Promise 77

Epilogue
Loving in the Dark 93

Introduction

One of the risks we take when we fall in love is discovering that our love has not been reciprocated with the same depth and breadth of commitment which we brought to the relationship. The older and more mature we are, the more painful such a discovery can be. The discovery is more than disappointing. It can leave us feeling alone, rejected, angry, foolish, maybe even fantasizing about running away to start life over. Love counts upon mutual commitment. Without commitment, without the assurance that the one, or the ones, whom we love will be there for us, it is nearly impossible to share ourselves fully. Without commitment — given, accepted, returned — we cannot love, we cannot live, with the freedom of the children of God. And when in a close relationship love and commitment become unbalanced, when expectations do not meet, when commitment is proffered but not accepted or accepted but not returned, then the stage is set for profound disappointment. Friendships collapse, marriages break down, community life becomes hollow. One feels betrayed — by one's friend, by life itself, or even by God for having created such a world or for not having intervened to save us from being hurt.

Promises are important. Not the half-meant promises of a love which has never been tested or the facile promises of a passing infatuation. Not the grandiose promises which go beyond human capability or the desperate promises born out of fear or insecurity. The promises which count are the fruit of falling in love; the promises which stretch toward an unseen future, in hope; the ones through which we commit ourselves, with all that we are, to someone. The kind of promise I mean is the readiness to throw in one's lot — one's very life — with another. It repeats itself, day by day, because this is the only way we can live: from one day to the next. Even the promise never to leave someone, to be faithful forever, can mean only as much as we are willing to invest in it day by day, for it is in the day-by-day that we do not abandon one another, that we struggle together, rejoice together, and together bear each other's burdens and listen to one another's fantasies and hopes. In the day-by-day, the forever of our promises becomes real. And yet the peace that we need in order to live from one day to the next would be terribly fragile if it were constantly plagued by the fear that tomorrow we might be abandoned. We have to rely on one another's promises because promises are the way by which we love in the dark. At times when the eye cannot see and the mind has trouble comprehending, promises are all we have to fall back on.

From the way I have been speaking about promises, it would be natural to think first of the promises which men and women make to each other in marriage. When people want to entrust themselves to each other, they make a promise. Ideally, because it reflects the fidelity of God, such a promise is made for life. Yet the marriage promise, apart from the exclusiveness of that relationship (which has more to do with the nature of marriage than the nature of promise), is but one kind. There are others. Even though it may not be explicitly uttered, there is an implicit promise which parents make to their children by the very fact that they bring them to life: a promise to love and to nurture, to teach and to support, in short, to be father and to be mother. There is also the promise which close friends make to one another. It too involves fidelity. It is uttered perhaps more by deeds than by words, but it is certainly a promise: to care, to be faithful, to accept and to love, to keep confidences, to suffer alongside, to forgive. This is what parents say to their children, and friends to each other, day by day.

There is also, of course, the promise which individuals make to a community — for example, at baptism — which is renewed at the Eucharist. There we promise to be for others either sisters or brothers, according to the radical way Jesus redefined family relationships: " 'Who are my mother and my brothers?' And looking around at those seated in the circle he said, 'Here are my mother

2

and my brothers. For whoever does the will of God is my brother and sister and mother' '' (Mark 3:33-35). Then, too, there is the promise which a community makes to each of its members, also given at baptism and renewed at the Eucharist. The community promises that one will not be making the journey of faith alone, that there will be companions, other disciples, who will walk the way with us, supporting us by their example, listening when we need to share, and reassuring us of God's forgiveness and abiding love. There is the implicit promise which someone makes to others when, for example, in response to the Spirit, he or she undertakes some form of human service or of ministry in the Church. It is a commitment to be available for others, to share with others one's emotional, spiritual, and physical energies, often at considerable sacrifice. It is the sort of promise that runs in and out of the story of Jesus and which lays the pattern of our discipleship.

Whatever form they take, promises are things of the Spirit; they always involve faith, hope, and love, the three virtues which orient us toward God. Faith: because to make a promise one must believe in oneself, one must believe in one's sister or brother, and one must accept the holy mystery which has fashioned us to be creatures who must learn how to love in the dark. Hope: because promises are born out of confidence and courage, and they enable us to face the future without fear or anxiety. Love: because promises are expressions of self-giving, and it is love, finally, which makes it possible for us to recommit ourselves from one day to the next.

Why do we make promises? What is it about ourselves that leads us to want to make a promise or to secure a promise from someone else? Why do lovers make each other promise things? Clearly, promises are a source of security. They help us to manage in a world which often shows itself to be unreliable, where relationships fail because commitment is weak, and where truth and integrity are sacrificed to fear and self-interest. Promises ground us, making it possible for our desires and hopes to take root in the real world and enabling our souls to grow, free from the fear of rejection. Counting on promises, we dare to do things because we trust that those who have made promises to us will be true to their word. We want to make promises because we want to give of ourselves, for promises are expressions and proofs of love. We make promises because we want to testify to the truthfulness in our hearts or to the firmness of our intentions. Sometimes promises degenerate into threats, as when someone swears to do evil or to punish. But the notion of promise is essentially positive; it is the intention to do something good. And so, relying on another's promise, we are surrendering to another's goodness. For goodness is the climate of life. Without an experience of the world's goodness mediated to us by the goodness of other human beings, without some reason to face life with hope, the human heart cannot breathe; the soul will not survive.

WHAT GOD HAS PROMISED US

There is, however, another side to human promises, and this is the story of God's promises to us. Scripture repeatedly refers to what God has promised, what God has sworn to do, or what God has guaranteed. The promises made by human beings are frequently responses to what God has initiated and promised first. In the case of God's promises, however, it would be better to think of God as making one promise, not many different ones, unless we prefer to think of God's first promise being made over and over again. God has promised to be with us, to be God for men and women — a God of people, a God who calls people to life. This is the promise of creation, spoken "in the beginning." It is the promise of covenant where divine faithfulness toward the people of Israel becomes the prototype of God's relationship with the whole human race. It is the promise of justice proclaimed so strongly through the mouths of the prophets. It is the promise of Jesus, the one who in flesh and blood became Emmanuel, that is, God-with-us. It is Jesus' promise to his disciples to be with them always (Matt 28:20). It is the promise of the Spirit, the abiding Presence in the minds and hearts of those who seek the kingdom of God. In every case, the divine promise is an affirmation and protection of life, for God is not a God of death — of oppression, injustice, hatred, decay — but a God of life; not a God of the dead, but of the living (Matt 22:32).

4

While the divine promise is one, like sunlight passing through a prism and refracting into many colors, that promise spreads and radiates through human experience. It is there, in our experience, that God's promise is perceived and becomes believable. In our personal lives, in our families and communities, in our living together and sharing life, the promise of God makes itself felt. If this were not so, then the story of Jesus or even the story of God's dealings with the people of Israel would not touch or speak to us. Unless a sense of life as promise were already churning in our thoughts and feelings, working through the intricacies of our experience from day to day, we would never be able to respond to the prompting of the Spirit.

THE IMPORTANCE OF REVERSING OUR PERSPECTIVE

Perhaps it could be argued that human beings make promises only because God, the Creator in whose image and likeness we have been fashioned, has been revealed to us as a God of promise, that is, as a God who has made a promise to us. In some secret, mysterious way the human heart relies on that promise each time it, too, reaches toward the future and guarantees its truthfulness and fidelity with a promise of its own. Our attempts to be faithful to our word, frequently so enfeebled by sin, are sustained and outmatched by the faithfulness of God who by creating us has pledged not to allow the precious gift of our lives to wind up in ruins. In other words, human beings can draw strength as they struggle to be faithful to their promises, by remembering the faithfulness of the God of promise.

The chapters which follow, therefore, are reflections on God's promises to us rather than on our promises to God. The reason for this reversal is something a Christian (or any man or woman of faith) would assent to at the outset, namely, that we are never more properly human than when we are contemplating God in whose image and likeness we have been created. The fact that we are God-oriented beings is what, essentially, both distinguishes and ennobles us. The human person is never more fully human — and more fully spiritual — than when he or she is attending to and in touch with the holy mystery of God. As a result, we want to consider *God's* promises because it is good for us to exercise

5

our contemplative sense, that inner sense which orients us outward and upward: out of ourselves, upward to the mystery of God. We do this when we meditate or pray, when we attend to the word of God in Scripture, or when we converse with others about things which truly matter. Many things in the world can draw us out of ourselves — stunning sunsets, the pounding of the ocean, the antics of children, the misfortune and suffering of our neighbors, or family celebrations. But not everything automatically puts us in contact with God. God is something further. God is the goodness behind all that we love; God is the love behind all that we care for. And it is God who looks at us from the desperate faces of the homeless or those fleeing political or social persecution, those who are starving or who languish in prisons or who are destitute. For this reason, we need faith and we need to pray: apart from prayer and faith we shall never learn how to perceive the ever-faithful God who meets us through ordinary human experience.

TO KNOW WHO WE ARE WE MUST START WITH GOD

All of our reflection about God vibrates between two poles or two questions. The first pole is the human one, and the question is, "What does it mean to be human?" Within the orbit of this pole, we reflect about what human beings mean when they make a promise; what happens when they fall in love; what prompts them to want to hope or to trust; or why they crave community. In other words, within the orbit of this reflection we attend to our experience. We listen to what our hearts, our minds, and our desires tell us about ourselves; and we gradually learn about how we were put together, that is, what makes us tick.

But we also know by faith that we have been made in the image and likeness of God (Gen 1:26-27). Consequently, the way we have been put together tells us something about the One who created us, the One whose image and likeness we bear. That is why there has to be a second pole, a second question: What is God like? This question is far more difficult to answer. It is much easier to concentrate upon our experience of ourselves and to think anthropologically rather than theologically, which anyone who has encountered distractions in prayer will appreciate. We may start our

6

praying by attending to God, but frequently we trail off by dwelling upon ourselves. We lose the divine thread amidst the cares and distractions of life. In other words, it is our slowness to become truly contemplative that makes it hard for us to know what God is really like, and not some obscurity or opaqueness about the divine mystery.

That is not to say that we cannot learn to be contemplative or that the things of everyday life are necessarily alien to the kingdom of God and God's concerns. Far from it. But it is one thing to find our souls absorbed by the cares of life and de-centered, and another thing to find God in all things. Everyday concerns distract us from God whenever the soul is not properly centered, that is to say, when the soul is either not sure or not clear about what truly matters in our lives. In order for the soul to be centered, it needs to develop the habit of noticing the presence and action of God in one's life. It needs to listen to what God is saying to us in Scripture, particularly through the gospels. Like Mary's sister Martha, the soul needs to learn how to choose the better part (Luke 10:38-42). Developing this habit involves mind, heart, and imagination. It leads to thinking — to seeing and understanding the world — contemplatively. It results in living within a God-centered perspective.

The foundational belief for all theological reflection is that no human reality can be adequately understood apart from the mystery of God. And since that mystery reveals itself within our experience, perhaps the major task of theology in every age is so to clarify people's experience that they realize and then celebrate the enduring presence of God in their lives. Should theology become so preoccupied with the human element that what God is like is allowed to drift to the margins of our consciousness, then theology becomes anthropology pure and simple. The divine dimension slips into a purified projection of the human. And this slippage happens relatively easily, too. People enjoy it when speakers, teachers, or writers help them to notice and interpret their own experience. Often such interpretations draw a great deal on psychological and sociological insights into human thinking and behavior, and the value of these insights should not be underestimated.

But this is not *all* theology does. Just as teachers not only try to illuminate experience but also to open students to brand new kinds of experience, so too theology does not merely attempt to explain experience. Theology also tries to open people's minds and hearts to something "ever ancient, ever new," namely, the wonder of the divine mystery. Many things in life are there for us to experience, but we simply have not been exposed to them. This is something every teacher realizes in the effort to introduce students to new concepts and ideas, or every parent realizes in the effort to get children to sample something they have not eaten before. The divine mystery is not something outside of our world and foreign to our experience, something fabricated and then offered to human beings for them to accept or reject. The divine mystery is deeply embedded in the texture of daily life: the feelings, encounters, events, doubts, relationships, activities, and concerns, in short, the stuff of a typical day in the lives of ordinary men and women. Our awareness of that mystery has to be cultivated and the experience of that mystery acknowledged. Otherwise the human spirit withers and dies.

Every human life is both gift and promise. The person who has acquired the habit of beholding life as a gift is in touch with that mystery of goodness which makes our believing, our hoping, and our loving possible. What we have already received, however, is a pledge to us that life, once given, will not be taken away. This is the great promise of God. This is the meaning behind the two great symbols of divine promise in Christian faith: creation and resurrection. Through these two great symbols, through these two great stories — the story of God's creating the world and the story of God's re-creating it in Jesus — one starts to grasp how all of life is a down payment on what is yet to come (see Romans 8).

PROMISES AS PRAYERS OF HOPE

Several years ago I published *Renewing the Baptismal Promises*. The book was written to assist those preparing for the Church's annual renewal of their baptismal commitment at the Easter Vigil to understand what they were assenting to when they made their profession of faith. There I tried to emphasize the practical consequences of Christian belief. Faith, after all, is not simply an affair of the head; faith calls us to live and act as followers of Jesus and as daughters and sons of God. That book might have had as its sub-theme "Our Promises to God." Incorporating that broader theme into the book would have relatively easy. It could be argued that every serious promise we make during our lives is ultimately made to God, since to dishonor one's promise is ultimately to dishonor God, who is both Life itself and Truth itself.

But as I have already remarked, every promise we make to God has another side to it. In and through whatever we promise God, God is also making a promise to us. Indeed, it could even be said that God's promise always comes first, in the form of grace, urging us to live boldly and faithfully as men and women of God. The inspiration which leads us to profess and to attempt great things, especially the great thing of parting with everything in order to gain our heart's desire (see Matt 13:44-45), comes from the Spirit. The divine promise is nothing less than the gift of God's own self. "Do this, *and you will live*" (Luke 10:28) is a promise of life: divine life, holy life, humanly fulfilling life, life according to the Spirit. If we did not somehow discern God's promise in the background of our lives, we would not have the basic hope and trust necessary to live as followers of Jesus from one day to the next.

Two points need to be made here. First, the context in which we make our Christian promises is always the Church, the community of believers; for the Church has learned over the ages what sort of promises truly expand our souls and our capacity to receive the breath of God. Some things which people might want to promise God in order to demonstrate the sincerity of their faith could ultimately prove harmful. Instead of heartening us, they would dishearten because they might not proceed from the Spirit. The Church's wisdom, patiently acquired over centuries of Christian practice, becomes an important safeguard against promises made with too much fervor and enthusiasm and with too little understanding of the ways of the Spirit.

Second, strictly speaking, a promise made to God is essentially a prayer of hope and trust. While it may be our intention to promise something or to commit ourselves to the Lord, these intentions always presuppose the grace and mercy of God: grace, because Christian experience knows that God always precedes our good intentions and the strength of God carries them along lest we fall; and mercy, because however strongly we insist or promise, Christian experience also reckons with human weakness, error, and failure. While we count on God's strength to sustain us, we also count on God's faithfulness to be with us when we fail, to heal our broken resolution, and to forgive. Human promises to God never presuppose perfection. Rather, they point to our desire for it. Promises orient us toward the future; they are basically prayers of hope. They bear witness to the natural yearning of the human heart to live before God with complete openness and freedom — never hiding, never running away, never fearing. In other words, promises are indirectly saying to God: "I want to be fully free, fully myself, and completely truthful. I want to live as You created me to be."

With these two points in mind, we return to the idea that for every promise we make to God, God is also promising something to us. The divine promise is nothing less than God's own self since God has promised to give himself to us. We likewise believe that the Spirit is the promise of God: Spirit as the life-giving source of our faith and hope; the animating breath that makes all human love possible; the silent, abiding Presence which steadies us from one day to the next, drawing us to want to be perfect as our heavenly Father is perfect (Matt 5:48). The Spirit is the promise of the Father and the Son (John 15:26) who gently enlarges our capacity to forgive, to share, to be honest, to pray. Perhaps when all is said and done, God *is* promise. That is, God is the future which can and will be ours if we allow ourselves to be led by the Spirit.

Human beings have been created for God. Our destiny is union with God and with one another, in and through the divine Spirit who is love itself. This destiny lies in front of us as possibility and as promise and is the true object of our hope. All human striving for community, for justice, for reconciliation, and for peace (themes which pervade Vatican II's Pastoral Constitution on the Church in the Modern World) springs from the ground of every human hope which is the mystery of God. We were created for communion, as everyone who has ever fallen in love readily com-

10

prehends. But the embrace we long for exceeds every human relationship imaginable. We long to be embraced by Life itself, and in that embrace we shall one day be united with every creature under heaven. That is why, even now, there are peacemakers on earth. That is why there are those who hunger and thirst for justice. And that is why the kingdom of God so captivates our imaginations. The Spirit of Jesus urges us forward, just as it drew him, to spend ourselves for the sake of justice and peace. To desire God is to long for the oneness of the human race and to share the divine passion which would bring this about.

THE ROLE OF THE STORY

By way of introduction, something probably ought to be added about the role of stories. While the Church presents Christian faith through its official doctrines and creeds, its faith is more forcefully and more attractively proclaimed through the great stories of salvation history which we find in the Bible. Today, perhaps more than ever before, the weight of this fact is coming home to us. We live, finally, by stories. We like to hear stories, we like to tell stories (especially our own), and we like to pass along the best of them to our children and grandchildren. Stories tie up life's loose ends. Even without our adverting to them, stories are what confer meaning upon our lives and upon our brief appearance within human history. Stories provide the imaginative reasonableness of the world as we experience it. In fact, not only do stories shape the way we experience the world; they also hold our world together by defining what is meaningful and what is not, what is valuable and what is not, what is of God and what is not.

Think for a moment about the stories we tell. Think about how we tell them and to whom we tell them. We have stories about our children, our parents, and our grandparents. We have chapters or episodes from our own personal histories, things which happened to us while we were growing up or in school, or just after we were married. There are stories about exotic places we may have visited, great personal or family crises; or chance meetings with a famous athlete or politician. There are stories about what it was like to live during the Great Depression or to serve in the Second World War. And for those whose lives have been closely associated with the Church, there might be stories of what it was like to live before the Second Vatican Council and the wonderful religious springtime which followed it.

In short, there are hundreds of stories, each one remembered and shared because it has been important in defining our time and place in history, each one important and memorable because it tells a little more about who and what we are. I have often thought, in fact, that human beings have been created by a master storyteller, and one of the effects of being made in that divine image and likeness is that we, too, crave to tell our stories. The only one, however, who really has both the time and the genuine interest to hear us through from beginning to end, who will ask the gentle questions that pry loose a sticky memory, challenge us when some detail is not making sense, or help us to see the deeper threads running through the individual chapters of our lives, is God. The fact of the matter is that we tell stories, and the truth is that our stories are nothing to be ashamed of. In the end, each human life can be the story of a promise kept. Only in the process of narrating it, however, are we likely to see how this has been so.

In the minds of some people, however, stories are not ultimately trustworthy. While acknowledging their role and importance in everyday life, they either suspect or discount the reliability of the grand stories out of which many of us live, namely, the scriptural stories which tell us about who we are and where we come from; about God's involvement with the human race and, in particular, with the story of Jesus. For many people today, there seems to be a crisis with respect to meaning and truth. Philosophy and metaphysics have, for the most part, disappeared as the conceptual bedrock for thinking and talking about the mystery of God and human transcendence. How does one prove that there really is a God, that existence is meaningful, that human history has a purpose, or that men and women have been created for union with Love itself? Is there some intrinsic reasonableness to the Easter story or is Easter merely a symbol of human hopefulness, a protest against every form of injustice? Why, in other words, should the story of Jesus be told and celebrated? Does it have a fundamental connection with the mystery of God such that the story of Jesus is also a story about God?

Indeed, the meaningfulness of the great Christian stories has been assaulted, critiqued, and "deconstructed." The result appears to be that we understand everything about them and we understand nothing. We know how and when they were composed. We know how to sort out fact from fiction, story from history, history from faith. But the more we have understood, the more difficult it has been for some people to locate and trust the transcendent dimension. Somehow, God seems to have disappeared from the reality of our living. The sense of the immediate presence of God which many once possessed, or which they eagerly sought after, seems either to have vanished or to have been proven to be illusory. And if that is the way things stand, more or less, with many people today, then what is the point of talking about divine promises? We can only be as certain of divine promises as we are certain of the reality of God.

In addition to the crisis of meaning, other factors have also contributed to our loss of the sense of the transcendent. The world's spiritual climate appears to have weakened, even as its life-protecting ozone layer continues being destroyed. Life according to the Spirit is threatened on every side by a practical atheism constantly bombarding us with a message totally at odds with the message of Jesus. By practical atheism I mean a way of living which effectively rejects the reality of God; it denies at the level of action or practice the great commandment: "Hear, O Israel! The Lord is our God, the Lord alone! Therefore, you shall love the Lord, your God, with all your heart, and with all your soul, and with all your strength" (Deut 6:4-5).

In the past, the Church's preaching was criticized for being too otherworldly. The Church was accused of turning people's gaze and imaginations away from this world toward heaven, thereby leading them to undervalue the present life in favor of life everlasting. At its worst, the consequence of this attitude, it has been suggested, was to prevent the followers of Jesus from being seriously engaged in the affairs of this world. They were slow to acknowledge and resist various forms of economic, social, and political oppression. Preoccupation with the next life prevented the followers of Jesus from confronting the dehumanizing forces of injustice in this world. Religion was simply a way of coping with the evil and unfairness which had to be endured in this valley of tears.

Needless to say, not only would such an attitude be profoundly un-Christian and false to the life and teaching of Jesus. It would also finally prove to be self-destructive. Anyone who concentrates so totally on the things of God that he or she prematurely separates from this world will eventually discover that it is not the living God whom he or she is following, but some idol, some false spirit seducing human beings into side-stepping the journey with Jesus. This sort of spirituality will never satisfy the human heart's longing for God, except by re-fashioning God to fit human dimensions.

Yet the fact remains that our culture's spiritual climate has grown thin. Our consumer culture does not seem to appreciate, let alone cultivate, the contemplative sense. This complaint is hardly new; it merely goes hand-in-glove with the materialism and careerism so characteristic of our part of the world. One further thinks about the fact that human beings appear less and less capable of making and keeping promises. One thinks of the wholesale breakdown of commitment and trust which are the underpinnings of life according to the Spirit. Lying, betrayal, perjury, deception, cover-ups: these may have become so prevalent that their contraries — truthfulness, integrity, courage, and honesty — have become the exception, and in some circles even unnatural. People are praised for being truthful and possessing integrity, as if society no longer expects that these virtues should be the foundation of human community. Greed, cowardice, and the pursuit of power have led to the erosion of that spiritual climate which alone makes community possible. As that climate has deteriorated, so too has the ability and the readiness of men and women to listen to the Word of the Lord. For the Lord is "faithful in all his words, and holy in all his works" (Ps 145:13). What characterizes every utterance of God is faithfulness. But how are people to experience, let alone trust, divine faithfulness when there is so much taking place in our culture that leads to distrust, to skepticism, or even worse, to an outright indifference about matters of honesty and truth?

All this has hurt our ability to hear God in the Christian story. No amount of infallible reassurances can repair the damage since authority too has suffered the consequence of being demythologized or deconstructed. Why should we listen to someone merely because that person occupies a position of authority? What guarantee do we have that the person, or the person's position, can reassure us of anything? That is why fundamentalist responses to a crisis of meaning are no help to men and women who reason, who raise critical questions, and who listen attentively to their experience of life and history. There is simply no human reality, no human voice or institution which can protect us from our doubts and questions about ourselves or about God. The history of human beings in this world is riddled with insecurity.

And yet, paradoxically enough, those who have come closest to knowing God have also discovered that this is the way things must be. God cannot be possessed, for it is God who gradually takes possession of us. Because we are, after all, only finite human beings, insecurity inevitably attaches itself to us. The insecurity we feel within ourselves and in the world around us will last until God finally and definitively holds us. Any way of coping with that insecurity which ignores or denies this essential truth serves only to increase our sense of being rootless and adrift. It merely decenters and destabilizes the soul further by stretching its loyalties and affections in every direction except toward God.

But no creature under heaven can stand in place of God. No person, no institution, no sacred book, no relationship can anchor us against the soul's deepest anxieties and questions: Do I count? Was I created by a loving God? Does my life have meaning? Is God real? For when all is said and done, our faith has to rest in God and God alone. Every created thing, each in its own way, points to God; but absolutely nothing can take God's place. Face to face with God, we stand alone — God and the soul.

Why, therefore, do we continually refer back to the Christian story? Why do we allow the gospels, for example, to shape our lives by supplying us with the images, the parables, and the lessons which govern the way we think and act and interpret our experience? Why have we allowed the story of creation to direct the way we look at the universe or the story of Jesus to govern how we understand and evaluate everything we do, everything we are and hope to be, and everything that happens to us?

The reason is that we have nothing else to turn to and depend upon apart from our stories. Stories are the building blocks of our worlds, at least of our inner worlds. Each of us is a storyteller, if only of that story which we know best because we have been living it firsthand. Story is all there is, but this realization is not a matter to which one simply resigns oneself because philosophy or science has failed to uncover the real, metaphysical truth of things. To put it another way, story is the metaphysical truth about us. We write stories, we live stories, we share stories because stories engage us as little else can. The God of Jesus does not come to us through a scientific theorem or through an abstract philosophical idea; this God comes to us through a story.

And why do we listen to that story? Maybe this invites the more basic question, why do we listen to any story? We listen to stories because we like them, and we like them best when they speak to our heart's desire. Is this something which we as part of a consumerist society have forgotten? Have we, even as adults, forgotten how to use our imaginations and to listen, contemplatively, to the stories which tell us who we are? Perhaps what we should really be thinking about, therefore, is what our hearts fundamentally want. It is this, I believe, which will bring us to realize that our natures — our selves — have been oriented towards God long before we ever gave God a thought. The mind, we eventually realize, is at home in the story of creation.

This much had to be said at the outset. In order to talk about God's promises, we have to turn to the great Christian stories. In doing so, we are not drawing on some make-believe world of religious fantasy. Rather, we are drawing upon the life-giving narratives which have sustained the Christian community down through the ages. The truthfulness of those stories is testified to precisely because they have been a source of life. Maybe one of them could even start like this: "In the beginning, God made a promise."

One final note. In the pages that follow, whenever I refer to

God as "he" or "his," I obviously do not mean that God has a gender, but only that the divine reality is personal. This accounts for the reason why the biblical writers referred to God by means of personal pronouns. In fact, because God is personal, it becomes possible for human beings to address God by name (e.g., Gen 4:26, 12:18; Exod 6:3). The effort to use non-sexist language when talking about the divine reality becomes cumbersome, particularly when one is dealing with familiar scriptural passages or when, following the practice of Jesus, one feels at home addressing God as Father (Luke 11:2; Rom 8:15), although, to be sure his is a God who is as much mother as father.

Chapter One

Creation as Promise

THE HISTORICAL EXPERIENCE OF CREATION AND PROMISE

There is no firmer place to begin reflecting upon God's promise than "in the beginning." After all, it is in the Bible's first story that Christian faith forms its picture of the relationship between God and the earth, between God and human beings, and between human beings and their world. God saw everything which had been created, was obviously pleased and gratified with the divine handiwork, and pronounced everything "good." That was the first and foundational blessing. Everything has been blessed from the very start of our history by the Creator. All subsequent blessings serve only to lay bare once again the original blessing which God pronounced.

But God did not simply create the world and then withdraw from its concerns, abandoning human beings to work things out for themselves. The creation of life had to be followed by the creation of history and the formation of a people. Yet not only does God create history; God also creates *in* history. God creates historically, for creation is an ongoing process, inextricably connected with all the events and experiences which make up our lives as individuals and as a race. The early books of the Bible show how the creative hands of God stretched into times and places. The creation of the people of Israel is continuous with the divine creative work "in the beginning." According to the biblical story, then, God continued to be involved with the lives and fortunes of the race which had just been created: Cain, the son of Adam, who killed his brother, sentenced to wander over the earth, yet protected by God's sign; Enoch, the one who walked with God; Noah and his family, spared from the great flood;

Abraham, the first one who put his faith in God and became the father of God's chosen people; Isaac, Jacob, and Joseph, the one who was sold by his brothers but whom God used to save the lives of many from starvation.

To some of them God made promises. With Noah, God made a covenant, forever recalled whenever a rainbow appears in the sky: "[Never] again shall all bodily creatures be destroyed by the waters of a flood; there shall not be another flood to devastate the earth. . . . As the bow appears in the clouds, I will see it and recall the everlasting covenant that I have established between God and all living beings — all mortal creatures that are on earth" (Gen 9:11, 16). To Abraham, God promised land and posterity: "The Lord, the God of heaven, who took me from my father's house and the land of my kin, and who confirmed by oath the promise he then made to me" (Gen 24:7).

The same promise was repeated to Jacob in a dream:

"And there was the Lord standing beside him and saying: 'I, the Lord, am the God of your forefather Abraham and the God of Isaac; the land on which you are lying I will give to you and your descendants. These shall be as plentiful as the dust of the earth, and through them you shall spread out east and west, north and south. In you and your descendants all the nations of the earth shall find blessing. Know that I am with you; I will protect you wherever you go, and bring you back to this land. I will never leave you until I have done what I promised you' " (Gen 28:13-15).

Finally, that divine promise took on special form and precise content when God made a covenant with the people of Israel at Mount Sinai after he had rescued them from slavery and oppression. This is beautifully summed up in Deuteronomy 30:15-20:

"Here, then, I have today set before you life and prosperity, death and doom. If you obey the commandments of the Lord, your God, which I enjoin on you today, loving him, and walking in his ways, and keeping his commandments, statutes, and decrees, you will live and grow numerous, and the Lord, your God, will bless you in the land you are entering to occupy. If, however, you turn away your hearts and will not listen, but are led astray and adore and serve other gods, I tell you now that you will certainly perish; you will not have a long life on the land which you are crossing the Jordan to enter and occupy. I call heaven and earth today to witness against you: I have set before you life and death, the blessing and the curse. Choose life, then, that you and your descendants may live, by loving the Lord, your God, heeding his voice, and holding fast to him. For that will mean life for you, a long life for you to live on the land which the Lord swore he would give to your fathers, Abraham, Isaac and Jacob.''

As one attends closely to the scriptural narrative, one starts to appreciate that God not only remained actively concerned about what happened to his creatures, particularly to his own especially chosen people, but that God also had an agenda or purpose in creating the human race. That purpose was more than biological; that is, God intended more for us than that we should simply increase, multiply, and fill the earth. The very fact that God took such care to prepare the earth with lakes and seas, with animals and fish, with all sorts of fruit-bearing plants and trees, not to mention the sun, the moon, and the stars by which human beings could see both by day and by night and be able to measure time and seasons, speaks a great deal to us about God's plan for the quality of life his creatures were to enjoy. Thus the Psalmist exclaims:

When I behold your heavens, the work of your fingers,
    the moon and the stars which you set in place —
What is man that you should be mindful of him,
    or the son of man that you should care for him?
(Ps 8:4-5)

In order that human beings should not be alone, God made us male and female. In other words, God also created family, friendship, and community life, for what good would all the material things of the earth be if the human being had to exist alone? What sort of creatures would we have been if we had been fashioned to dwell in this world either alone inwardly, in our minds and souls, or alone externally and socially, without companionship, language, and most of all, without love? As Christian faith teaches, even God does not exist in eternal isolation. We might even wonder further what sort of world God would have made if a genuine community of nations were a completely unrealistic hope or if the human race were perpetually trapped by hostility, national arrogance, and division. Phrasing the question this way enables us to see that in no way could such a state of affairs be the result of God's design. It would not conform to the creation story. And it would certainly not conform to the story of Jesus through whom, as Paul tells us, "God was reconciling the world to himself" (2 Cor 5:19).

TWO FUNDAMENTAL TRUTHS

The creation story begins to reveal divine purpose and plan. It becomes increasingly evident, as we move further along, that God stands for and defends certain values, the two most notable of which are the creature-creator relationship itself and the dignity or worth of life. Thus we read: "I, the Lord, am your God, who brought you up out of the land of Egypt, that place of slavery. You shall not have other gods besides me" (Exod 20:2-3). And again: "For your own lifeblood, too, I will demand an accounting: from every animal I will demand it, and from man in regard to his fellow man I will demand an accounting for human life" (Gen 9:5). The biblical conviction about our having been created by a God who would rescue people from slavery and protect human life gives rise to two fundamental truths which are correlative to the divine promise.

The first truth is that human beings are not properly themselves unless they are living out their relationship with God. God is their Creator, the source of their life, a fact which is reaffirmed each time they breathe. As such, God deserves unqualified obedience. That is to say, God must be listened to with open, generous hearts, for not to listen to God is to court disaster. Not to listen to the Creator is to risk injuring or even losing one's humanity. Besides, the creature is being asked to render obedience to a Creator whose motive in fashioning the world was love. God was not creating human beings to be robots or automatons. Rather, they were fashioned after the divine image and likeness itself, creatures with minds and hearts, destined to live and enjoy the earth together, in community. They were created by love and for love.

Obeying God, then, is hardly demeaning, even for a sophisticated age like ours; obedience to the Creator is not an insult to human maturity and independence. Listening to God is the pathway to life, for the voice of God leads to freedom. The God who delivers from slavery is a God who does not want people enslaved thereafter by anything. But the only way to guarantee this liberty is to make sure that human beings do not surrender their loyalty and their freedom to any false god.

The second truth is this: Precisely because it comes from God who gives life because God is life, human life deserves the utmost respect. While the Bible reports many episodes about God's taking the side of Israel in its bloody wars against its neighbors, it is also clear, as one reads further, that biblical theologies grow more subtle as writers fathom more deeply what God's concerns truly are. Eventually, at least some biblical authors realize that God's providential care for the world and the human race is far more universal than many in Israel could either comprehend or appreciate. By the time we come to the prophet Isaiah, we notice that the divine attention is firmly directed toward all nations and peoples, not exclusively toward the nation of Israel: "On that day Israel shall be a third party with Egypt and Assyria, a blessing in the midst of the land, when the Lord of hosts blesses it: 'Blessed be my people Egypt, and the work of my hands Assyria, and my inheritance, Israel'" (Isa 19:24-25). The prophetic literature affirms that the quality of every human life has to be protected by laws which clearly reflect God's burning concern for justice and God's compassion for those who are defenseless or unfairly deprived of their rights.

The year of jubilee — during which all debts were to be forgiven, fields were to be restored to their original owners, Hebrew slaves were to be set free, and even the land itself was to be given a rest from planting and harvesting — testifies to the divine preoccupation with justice, mercy, and freedom (see Lev 25). The sabbatical rest from work — for human beings, for animals, and for the earth — revealed that work and productivity were not life's absolute value in the sight of the Creator. Through the Law, God made it abundantly clear how human beings were expected to live in community. What secured everything was the relationship between Creator and creature, whereby the creature daily acknowledged God's goodness and sovereignty and constantly recalled the marvelous things which God had done.

In creating the heavens and the earth, God had implicitly made a promise to Adam and Eve, and to all of their descendants. Forever, the human race would belong to God; its good would be God's overriding concern. This is the substance of the divine promise. If history failed — that is, if the human race were to elect wickedness over holiness, falsehood over truth, greed over justice, and idolatry over faith — then that failure would reflect badly upon the Creator. God could not afford that kind of moral collapse, for then one might wonder whether the Creator knew what he was doing in fashioning the world. This sort of reasoning, apparently, was exactly what was on Moses' mind when he responded to God's decision to wipe the people out:

"Are the Egyptians to hear of this? For by your power you brought out this people from among them. And are they to tell of it to the inhabitants of this land? It has been heard that you, O Lord, are in the midst of this people; you, Lord, who plainly reveal yourself! Your cloud stands over them, and you go before them by day in a column of cloud and by night in a column of fire. If now you slay this whole people, the nations who have heard such reports of you will say 'The Lord was not able to bring this people into the land he swore to give them; that is why he slaughtered them in the desert'" (Num 14:13-16).

No, there would be no way for God to protect the divine investment, as it were, apart from being involved with human history. Thus, by means of the great flood which cleansed the earth, God corrected the wickedness which had inserted itself into creation. Later, after pledging never to resort to that sort of intervention again, God would work through everyday realities, through political and social events, to recall human beings to faith and to justice. Sometimes that spelled military defeat and the humiliation of captivity in a foreign land. At other times, it might mean famine and drought or the scourging voice of prophets. Whatever form it took, divine care for the integrity of creation — for the moral, spiritual survival of the human race — kept erupting into history, thereby making history not just a chronicle of what happened to human beings over the ages, but the story of their salvation as well.

What then do we learn from all of this? First and foremost, we learn about divine faithfulness. The emerging picture of God reveals that God does not abandon creation. Rather, God even accompanies his people on their historical journey. This is dramatically symbolized in the Exodus story through the divine presence which associated itself with the holy dwelling or tabernacle, the ark of the covenant, and the pillar of fire by night and the cloud by day.

It is important for us today not to be so distracted by some of the narrative details that we lose sight of the elementary conviction about God to which they give rise. Whether or not there actually was a garden of Eden, or a great flood and a Noah's ark; whether or not there literally was a pillar of fire and manna from heaven, or a great crack in the earth which swallowed up the idol-seeking and faithless Israelites who had left Egypt with Moses, may not really be to the point. Not only are these particular stories ancient, but their form and content have also been shaped by constant re-telling. Like all stories, the re-telling has led to exaggeration and the introduction of dramatic effect. So too with the account of the plagues which God visited upon the Egyptians because of the hardness of Pharaoh's heart.

But what is not forgotten in these stories is God's determination to lead the people of Israel out of slavery and oppression into a Promised Land where they would be free — religiously, politically, economically. They would worship as they wished (that is, as the Lord had directed them). Identifying the Lord in their prayer as the one who rescued the people of Israel from cruel bondage is a constantly recurring scriptural refrain. They would no longer be subject to the tyranny of a foreign ruler. They would possess their own land to raise crops and herds, to build homes and villages, and to create secure futures for their children. What is not forgotten is the divine care that the people of God should not starve or be without leadership or be forced to survive without moral and spiritual guidance. What is not forgotten is God's approachability or the divine defense of the poor or the periodic outpourings of divine compassion and forgiveness, despite the harsh traits which often appear in the biblical narratives' depictions of God.

The self-revealing God of the Bible is a God who makes promises, who often guarantees what has been promised by swearing an oath, and who, no matter how angered he becomes as a result of Israel's frequent lapses into infidelity, always remembers his promises. Divine faithfulness was always greater than human failure, and in some paradoxical fashion, human infidelity served to highlight all the more brilliantly the faithfulness of God, an observation which Paul would make in his Letter to the Romans. "Where sin increased," Paul wrote, "grace overflowed all the more" (5:20). Human sinfulness provides proof of God's righteousness (3:5); "God delivered all to disobedience, that he might have mercy upon all" (11:32).

Creation itself is the primary symbol of divine promise, far more so than the rainbow which appeared in the sky after the great flood. "God has promised": what this means is that God is ready to stand *by* creation and *with* creation in such a way that human beings will never be abandoned. God is "there," to strengthen, to encourage, to forgive, to guide, to bless, to assist, and to struggle alongside his people. From time to time, the people experienced God's absence. The voice of the divinely designated leader or of the prophet disappeared from the land. At the same time, the people would suffer humiliating military defeat or drought and famine or exile in a foreign land. And yet, such events usually served the divine purpose of recalling the people to faith. Somehow the divine withdrawal creates a desert within the human spirit. The soul experiences such a disorienting thirst that it might not even be aware, in its delirious state, about what exactly it longs for:

Yes, days are coming, says the Lord God,
    when I will send famine upon the land:
Not a famine of bread or thirst for water,
    but for hearing the word of the Lord.
Then they shall wander from sea to sea
    and rove from the north to the east
In search of the word of the Lord,
    but they shall not find it.

26

On that day, fair virgins and young men
  shall faint from thirst.
(Amos 8:11-13).

But the divine absence prepared the way for God to become present again, more tenderly, more mercifully than ever before.

And why should God keep behaving this way? Why bother so much with an erring, faithless, and stiff-necked people? Because God remembers. God never forgets the promise, a promise not so much to keep forgiving as to keep creating, that is, to continue fashioning men and women into the image and likeness of God. Day in and day out, God does whatever is necessary for us to become fully daughters and sons of God. Indeed, the work of creating a fully human being takes a lifetime. God created the human race, ultimately, to be joined in love with the Creator. Promise recalls purpose, and the purpose behind it all is union. Creation, then, is a kind of sacrament, continually inviting us to remember why we have been made. The point is not that all creatures, one way or another, lead to the Creator, which would be the same as saying that all created things testify to the existence of God. That much has been said many times and in many different ways throughout the centuries. The point we are registering here, however, is not so much about God's existence, but about God's promise. In the psalms, for example, God is praised for creation. Once again, it is not that the Psalmist, inspired by wonder over what is to be seen in the world, is led to infer the existence of God. Rather, the Psalmist already accepts the fact of God's existence. Moved with wonder by what he sees in the created universe, the Psalmist is drawn to marvel at divine goodness and faithfulness, and to utter a prayer of thanksgiving.

THE DARK SIDE OF CREATION

Now, there is one great stumbling block to accepting this idea of praising God for the goodness of creation; it is what we might call the dark underside of creation. The fact is that we are confronted with the reality of death. Death's dark shadow spreads itself over everything, almost as if it were boasting of its power to bring us down. Death achieves this victory over human confidence about divine goodness, first and foremost, by tricking us into regarding our dying as evil. And for the sinful human being, that probably is the natural way to think about death: death is evil because it spells the end of life.

Yet the fact that things die is a property of all creation, which God has blessed. To be sure, the creation story tells us that death will be the penalty for Adam and Eve's disobedience: "You shall not eat it or even touch it, lest you die" (Gen 3:3). And Paul picked up on this point: "Through one person sin entered the world, and through sin, death, and thus death came to all. . . ." (Rom 5:12). But I think that there can be a reading of the story which would uncover fear as the real penalty, rather than death: "I heard you in the garden; but I was afraid, because I was naked, so I hid myself" (Gen 3:10). And this would also conform to something which Paul, possibly with this text in mind, said: "For you did not receive a spirit of slavery to fall back into fear. . . ." (Rom 8:15). Perhaps the creation story is simply telling us that God had threatened Adam and Eve with *their deaths*, that is, with being cut off from life prematurely, rather than with death itself, if they disobeyed.

If death itself had been the penalty for sin, then one might expect to find biblical writers lamenting the tragic loss of unending life. Instead, their usual lament is the loss of length of days since Scripture seems to accept death as part and parcel of God's providential arrangement of things; a long life, on the other hand, is a sign of divine blessing. We should add that for Christians the Easter story does not really undo the fact of death; death remains. Death's sting, however, is rendered harmless (1 Cor 15:55) because the fear which first gave rise to humanity's alienation from the Creator has been overcome.

I think it can be said, therefore, that in terms of the creation story death itself is not a disorder. It becomes so when linked to being afraid of God: death becomes fearsome and thereby exercises dominion over us, which ultimately gives sin its power; fear arises because of sin. For sin is the creature's running away and hiding from God's sight (as if this were possible), and we are terrified that God might find us. In the end, of course, God does go out looking for us; day by day, God goes out. God's fidelity to creation — to the divine promise — demands this. Christian faith refers to this going-out of God as the mystery of human redemption from sin. The prophet Ezekiel expressed this mystery beautifully: "I myself will pasture my sheep; I myself will give them rest, says the Lord God. The lost I will seek out, the strayed I will bring back, the injured I will bind up, the sick I will heal" (Ezek 34:15-16).

Besides death, however, there is the equally mysterious reality of suffering, particularly the suffering of innocent people and the suffering that results from injustice. Many people today (among them, many young people) do not believe in God. While atheism is hardly new to human history, the wholesale dismissal of religious belief and the reality of God seems to be gaining an ever wider acceptability. There was a time when not to believe in God was considered the height of presumption and irrationality; the existence of God seemed so demonstrably clear and intelligible that only an idiot would deny it: "The fool says in his heart, 'There is no God'" (Ps 14:1). Today, the opposite appears to be the case. Not believing in God appears to make more sense than believing, and the greatest single weapon in the atheist's armory is the experience of evil, suffering, and injustice. Who else bears ultimate responsibility when, for example, so many children have been abandoned to survive on the streets of South Africa, or Colombia, or Brazil? In modern times, the suffering endured by countless men, women, and children, many of them innocent victims of war, racial prejudice, and human greed, practically stuns the Christian apologist into silence. How does one dare to talk about — let alone preach — God's love and mercy in the face of such horrible tragedy? How do we console the parents of a son or daughter who has committed suicide, or the mother watching her child die from cancer, or the family shattered by poverty and ethnic violence?

Some Christians have proposed to answer the atheistic challenge by appealing to the fact of Jesus' death upon the cross as a victim of injustice. The Son of God also suffered, although he was innocent. The Son of God joined the ranks of the innocent voices throughout the ages who have cried out to God and were answered by the divine silence: "My God, my God, why have you forsaken me?" (Mark 15:34). What commends this answer is that it shows the issue to be far more complex than the atheistic challenge realizes, because it introduces suffering into God. The believer refuses to juxtapose divine goodness and human misfortune, as if every instance of human tragedy served to make faith in God's loving kindness less credible. In other words, according to the Christian story, God is drawn into and, in some mysterious way, even shares human suffering.

Scripture itself, of course, is hardly naive in the matter of divine goodness. While one could marshal an impressive array of texts which profess, in the most uncertain terms, the conviction about God's goodness and steadfast love, one could also appeal to many other texts which complain about the absence of God or God's apparent impotence or the success and prosperity of the unrighteous or the misfortune which befalls upright, innocent people. The Bible is unable to formulate a satisfying theological answer to the problem of evil. It acknowledges the reality of evil, yet at the same time it continues to assert its belief in God's faithfulness to his promises and steadfast love. The Christian answer begins a little differently, since it takes its point of departure from the Cross. The story of Jesus becomes a story of God. Thus, God "knows" suffering in his Son. Divine goodness did not prevent the emergence of sin, for sin was one of the consequences of our having been endowed with free will. Nor did divine goodness prevent innocent men and women from becoming victims of injustice. If anything, by gracing some individuals with zeal for justice and by allowing them to share the divine passion for human liberation so that they actively resisted what was unjust, God has actually contributed to their fate.

The result is that our experience of the world leaves us unsettled. On the one hand, we experience creation as good and as gift; on the other hand, we also experience its underside, as it were, where natural disasters occur, where human beings succumb to disease and death — often prematurely — and where countless lives are scourged by hunger and oppression. In what way can it be said, therefore, that God keeps his promise to us? What exactly has God promised? How can God be trusted?

The issue, it must be admitted, is perhaps the thorniest problem which most of us ever face as we struggle to lead lives of faith.

30

One is tempted either to throw up one's hands in a gesture of to-
tal renunciation or, with head bowed, simply and humbly to acknowledge God's sovereignty over creation while developing the
attitude of holy resignation: "God's will be done." Or else one
can travel through life keeping alive some faith in God (for the alternative of there not being a God at all appears so unthinkable),
while all along, plagued by nagging doubts about what kind of
God he is, one strains to decipher the reality of evil. Yet evil
simply stares back, like a gaping hole of horrifying blackness. As a
final alternative, one can simply give up believing altogether; non-
belief seems more plausible and less of a strain on one's intelli-
gence than belief.

RECONCILING DIVINE PROMISE WITH OUR EXPERIENCE OF EVIL

It is important, therefore, that each of us spells out exactly what
our experience and conception of God are. The reason, I believe,
that we pick up conflicting signals about the nature of God in our
experience is that we probably have not allowed our minds
enough room to think of God adequately. Our *idea* of God may be
too rigid or too abstract, while at the same time we may have
failed to notice exactly what our *experience* of God has been. Our
minds may be telling us one thing, while our experience wants to
report something different. Within the Bible, too, we can distin-
guish the various *conceptions* of God from the more fundamental
experiences of God. Scripture, for example, does not operate with a
purified notion of God. It would be a mistake to think that all the
biblical writers subscribed to and shared a theologically correct notion of God which always lay concealed behind some of their an-
thropomorphic representations of the divine reality. Was God
actually threatened, for example, by the fact that Eve and Adam
ate the forbidden fruit? Was God really disturbed by the tower
construction project at Babel? Did God need to rest after six days
of labor? Did God really go around fulminating against the people
of Israel when they wandered away and broke their side of the
covenant?

Indeed, the Bible does often depict God on a human scale; God
appears to react to events and behavior as a super-powerful, yet

still human being might. Most of us would probably feel com-
pelled to add, however, that clearly God is absolutely transcendent. God is the infinitely powerful, changeless, and eternally
loving Creator. And yet, precisely because that is the conception
of God most of us have inherited, we cannot figure out why such
a God allows so much evil. To suggest that God made us free,
that in the long run it is for our good that God respect that freedom, even when in the process we hurt ourselves and others,
does not conduct us very far, especially if we belong among the
innocent ones who have paid the price for another individual's
sinful exercise of his or her freedom. Nor does it help very much
to suggest that, while in this life many things are unfair, in the
next life God will straighten everything out, rewarding the just for
their goodness and loyalty, and punishing the wicked.

The critical question we have to ask is how God has disclosed
himself to each one of us, personally. Have we experienced God
as caring, deeply concerned — indeed, even in love with us — or
not? Does our experience confirm that God is a God of mercy and
love? Do we experience ourselves as men and women constantly
being created? Do we sense the faithfulness of God within our experience of ourselves and the world? Does that faithfulness sometimes express itself in terms of sensing oneself blessed or forgiven,
or mysteriously feeling in one's own soul the brokenness and poverty of the world and its cry over injustice? To repeat, the only
way to reconcile divine promise with our experience of evil is
from within our experience of God. We cannot work this out in
the abstract because God does not exist in the abstract. God exists
historically, in concrete relationships with men and women. The
notion of God in the abstract is like the notion of human nature in
the abstract. Human nature, in the abstract, does not exist; neither
does the divine mystery.

There is a properly Christian way of viewing the problem of evil
and suffering, and in the end this way does involve the Cross.
The Cross does not erase evil, however; if anything, it reaffirms
its existence under the form of injustice. An innocent man is arrested on trumped-up charges, tried illegally, brutally tortured,
and shamefully executed as a political subversive: and this man
was none other than the Son of God! In a way, the Cross is a

submission to the power of evil, yet the crucified one submits without ever renouncing his faith in God's passion for justice and God's oneness with the human race. There may be no theoretical solution to the problem of evil, but there is a practical one. For on the practical level, one converses with God about the experience of evil and suffering. With whom else would we speak? Job spoke with his friends (who were not all that helpful), but his wish was to address God and lay out his case because he sensed God had violated his rights. In other words, reconciling oneself with evil and suffering is a personal matter between the believer and God, and only in that context will one discover the proper light to view one's experience and the necessary hope to continue living. As far as I can determine, the only way to come to terms with our experience is through a personal relationship with God: a God who mysteriously speaks to us from the Cross of his Son. Friends can listen to us and share their own experience with us, but in the end they cannot speak for God.

THREE PERSPECTIVES ON CREATION

In the matter of understanding creation, there are a number of perspectives one might adopt. A person could subscribe to the idea that, as it came from God's hands, creation was good, but human sinfulness damaged that primordial goodness and order, causing us to lose that initial condition of grace and fall prey to all manner of suffering. This view of things, however, is not very helpful because it casts the mystery of redemption in the wrong light. Redemption was not a divine afterthought, as if God had to figure out what to do next after Adam and Eve sinned, and their descendants after them.

One might also view creation as still unfolding. In this case, it becomes unfair to judge God's creative work by what we see now, as we survey the present or review the past, because the work is unfinished. According to the biblical narrative, God saw that everything he made was good. It does not say that God made everything perfect or that creation (at least from a human stand-point) was flawless. While I would never argue that human suffering in and of itself is good, I believe, as the Church does, that good can come out of suffering. Yet this very possibility is itself a mark of divine wisdom. Neither suffering nor death is capable of erasing the Creator's blessing upon the world. This helps to explain why Paul could write, "We know that all things work for good for those who love God" (Rom 8:28). Since God is still creating the world, that is, since God is still bringing forth goodness, one will not finally be able to assess whether or not the divine plan has succeeded until the end of time. Only then will we know whether the divine creative intention has been realized. God's purpose in creating us, we believe, is union: all of us, in God, forever joined by the bond of divine love which is our life. But there is still a long way to go before that happens. The freedom of many people will need to be redeemed and transformed.

Still another possibility is that the creation story itself is less about the past than about the future. It proceeds from a dream about how things might be, and then reads that dream backwards, into history. We perceive creation to be flawed precisely because we have some idea as to how things might yet be, not how they once were. And sensing how they might be, we can also work to change the way things are so that the world conforms to human hope. Humanity's initial oneness with the Creator, so beautifully symbolized by God's moving about in the garden in the cool of the day looking for Adam (Gen 3:8-10), is the precious object of human hope, not of human memory and regret. If that is so, then the divine promise has to be read as a people's inspired hope rather than as a divine guarantee that everything in the present will go well for us if only we obey the commands of the Lord.

Yes, God is on the side of justice. Yes, the God we know is a God of mercy and compassion. But what God has promised us is God's own self. Yes, God is a liberating God, the one who would free human beings from their prisons and oppression, their hatred and lack of faith. This God will walk with us, empowering us and pointing the way, but that does not guarantee that here and now everything will become perfect. For Christians, the primary illustration of this fact is the story of Jesus. At the end of his life, the kingdom of God had not arrived. Neither the world nor the small region of it where he lived had suddenly become free from the power of sin. Yet this has not prevented countless men and women throughout the centuries from following him. And the reason is that, for Christians, the promise of creation is inseparable from the resurrection which we shall be looking at shortly. Maybe even Jesus did not have an exhaustive insight into the range of God's designs for the world, which extended beyond Galilee and Judea and the holy city of Jerusalem, to the farthest reaches of the earth and the most remote corners of history.

BACK TO THE QUESTION

To return to our question, we ask again: What has God promised and how has God been faithful to creation? God has promised us God's own self; but, I would suggest, whether or not that promise will be fulfilled can only be answered at the end of the human story, not at the beginning or in the middle. What we rely upon now are simply clues, intuitions, and inklings. And right now, in the present, there are men and women who have experienced this self-giving of God. They have found the clues; they know what God is like; they, too, have made promises.

In the end, perhaps it can be said that the divine promise corresponds to what we genuinely hope for, that is, to the hope which each of us carries in our hearts regarding the integrity or value of life itself. God has promised that our hope will be fulfilled. The divine promise, as revealed to us in Scripture, objectifies and puts into words all that our hearts long for and our souls desire. The problem of evil, as I remarked, is perhaps the most unyielding question that our experience can pose to faith. It is extremely difficult to reconcile God's promise with our present experience, unless we adopt the perspective that the promise is not meant to be fulfilled until the future. God's promise, in other words, is Scripture's way of verbalizing the most profound human hope.

Nevertheless, human beings have to work out their salvation in this world, a world which God pronounced good but which frequently shows itself to be imperfect and flawed. One would also like to be able to count on God's blessing here and now, and to experience the reassurance and strength which comes from trusting that even here and now God's promise will be fulfilled. Faith in God's goodness ought to come fairly easily to those who are already numbered among the fortunate ones of this world. Having been blessed with so much in terms of material goods, education, sound health, and secure families, it would seem that they, above all, should find the road to faith a smooth one. After all, they do enjoy, here and now, what many would regard as the fruit of God's promise.

Oddly enough, however, this often proves not to be the case. Instead of bolstering faith and purifying the interior life, affluence and security frequently have precisely the opposite effect. Where religion is present in such lives, it generally functions as a kind of ideological superstructure. That is, religion for such people becomes merely a way of explaining (and defending) the way things are. The gospel narrative becomes merely a pious story about a generous man who inspires us with his teaching and example, but the truly radical and challenging elements of his story are either overlooked or forgotten. Such people only begin to take their religious beliefs seriously when they are caught by the problem of evil. The sudden occurrence of evil in otherwise tranquil and materially secure lives prompts a great personal struggle of mind, heart, and soul. This happens because the problem of evil undercuts all facile, unquestioned beliefs about the nature of God and what God apparently owes us. The problem of evil, in short, is more of a problem for those whose faith is superficial than for those whose lives have been seasoned by some form of suffering.

This is not to imply that religion functions as an emotional crutch for lives hopelessly blocked economically, culturally, or socially, or for people who have had to endure a great deal of pain. That can happen, of course; the charge that religion merely aids weak people to make it through life is hardly new. Genuine faith, however, is altogether different. In faith, one meets God; one experiences the closeness of the holy mystery which both creates and sustains us. Historically, this is one advantage the poor have always had over the rich; the poor have been forced to survive at the edge, as it were. Reduced to approaching life in terms of the most basic human needs and goals, they have never faced the reality of evil as an abstract problem or a theoretical concern crashing into their world all at once. One reason why men and women from various spiritual traditions have embraced the ascetical practice of poverty, in fact, is precisely to capitalize on a truth of fundamental importance. God alone matters; everything else is necessarily secondary for those whose hearts belong to the kingdom of God. But whereas spiritually minded people make a choice to be poor, the truly poor of this world have this option thrust upon them, usually as a result of injustice, oppression, and neglect from the societies around them.

The reality of evil will not cease to exist; the problem of evil as a challenge to the promise of creation will not go away. But, as I have suggested, there is a spiritual resolution to the problem, and it involves faith: not faith as an either/or response to the world, as if one simply elects to believe in God because the alternative would render life intolerable, but faith as a profound grasp of the intricacy and the basic simplicity of life. The way of faith is itself persuasive. Men and women who are believers know why they believe, even when the world confronts them with its dark underside. For the way of faith is lifegiving.

What does believing do? How does it affect and transform the human mind and heart? Believing, as opposed to non-belief, shapes us into a particular kind of human being, one who spends his or her life in a fully conscious, trusting relationship with the silent, holy mystery of God. What does hope do? How does hoping affect and transform the human mind and heart? Hoping, as opposed to not-hoping and despair, molds us into a particular kind of person, too, one who faces life out of a conviction of life's goodness, its transcendent worth, and the ultimate triumph of justice. And what does loving do? How does loving change the human mind and heart? Far more than anything else, love has the power to transform us into the kind of human beings that we earnestly want to be. Love, contrary to hatred or revenge, transforms the human soul in the direction of compassion.

We are, of course, talking about the three theological virtues, as the reader has no doubt guessed. Faith, hope, and love are called theological virtues (they might equally well be called the three humanizing virtues) because they both originate with God and terminate in God. In the course of this going-out and returning, the human being is gradually formed into the divine image and likeness. Because God is love, the human being will not be fully fashioned into the divine likeness until it, too, loves as God loves: freely, selflessly, universally. This ongoing creation of the human person does not take place, however, apart from believing and hoping in God. But this truth can only be discovered experientially. We shall never know what faith and hope do to us apart from their practice.

The person who believes, who hopes, and who loves knows intuitively why the way of faith is the properly human way to live. Such is the way to freedom and peace. Only from within this way can one comprehend that evil is not so much a problem as a fact. As a fact, it must be faced and dealt with, but the person of faith never faces and deals with evil apart from God.

Is God faithful? Can God be trusted to keep his promise? For those who know God and have experienced the closeness of the divine mystery, the answer might take the form given by the Psalmist:

The Lord is faithful in all his words
    and holy in all his works. . . .
The Lord is near to all who call upon him,
    to all who call upon him in truth.
He fulfills the desire of those who fear him,
    he hears their cry and saves them.
(Ps 145:13b,18-19)

CHRISTIAN SELECTIVITY IN READING SCRIPTURE

Before concluding this chapter, it might be useful to add a note about why a Christian approaches the biblical texts selectively. Our understanding of God draws selectively upon various parts of Scripture, for after coming to know Jesus, the Christian reader cannot avoid viewing the Bible apart from the lens of the Gospel. Our conception of God and our access to God have been shaped by the gospels; the way we think about and imagine God has been deeply (and possibly irreversibly) affected by the story of Jesus. The Christian imagination, properly formed and nurtured, produces a picture of God which is consonant both with our experience and with the gospel narrative. As a result, when we read the Old Testament, our attention is going to fasten on some aspects of the Bible's way of speaking about God, while we either ignore or dismiss others.

This point deserves mention because there are many Christians who do not know quite how to react to some of the stories and narratives which appear in the Old Testament. They have been told that the Bible is the Word of God, and yet clearly much of what is said there is either irrelevant to their experience or leaves them bewildered. This is particularly the case when the Bible speaks about God in ways which do not seem to match the God of Christian imagination. Nevertheless, they recognize the danger of picking and choosing their way through Scripture, for who is to say what is to be accepted or rejected? That is why, of course, the Bible's proper interpretative space is always the community of believers, the Church. One depends upon teachers and preachers who both know Scripture well and are adequately versed in the tradition in which Scripture has been read and explained over the centuries.

Jesus would have read Scripture selectively, too. His imagination and heart, like ours, would have inclined more toward one book or passage over others, judging from the Old Testament citations and allusions which are attributed to him by the gospel writers. The way Jesus speaks about God does not at all points agree with what we find in the Old Testament. Notice the contrast, for example, between Deuteronomy 21:18-21 and Luke 15:11-32. The Old Testament text reads:

"If a man has a stubborn and unruly son who will not listen to his father or mother, and will not obey them even though they chastise him, his father and mother shall have him apprehended and brought out to the elders at the gate of his home city, where they shall say to those city elders, 'This son of ours is a stubborn and unruly fellow who will not listen to us; he is a glutton and a drunkard.' Then all his fellow citizens shall stone him to death. Thus shall you purge the evil from your midst, and all Israel, on hearing it, shall fear."

But Jesus, in the parable of the runaway son who squandered his inheritance on loose living, draws the picture of a father who treats the lost son very differently: "Then let us celebrate with a feast, because this son of mine was dead, and has come to life again; he was lost, and he has been found."

Knowing what the Law of Moses had ordained, how could Jesus dare to create such a story? Or again, after reading the precise regulations governing cultic worship in the Books of Exodus, Leviticus, and Numbers, one has to be struck by the radical statement of Jesus in John's Gospel to the Samaritan woman at Jacob's well: "Believe me, woman, the hour is coming when you will worship the Father neither on this mountain nor in Jerusalem. . . . [The] hour is coming, and is now here, when true worshipers will worship the Father in Spirit and truth; and indeed the Father seeks such people to worship him" (John 4:21, 23). Here, Jesus has set aside Israelite cult and temple worship and replaced it with something altogether different, at least as far as externals were concerned. And of course, the same sort of selectivity occurred in the Sermon on the Mount when Jesus said, "You have heard that it was said to your ancestors. . . . But I say to you . . . ." (Matt 5:21-22).

Perhaps the most striking example of selectivity (and diversity) is the contrast between John the Baptist and Jesus. Behind each figure there seems to lie very different experiences of God. John was the classic prophet, perhaps like another Jeremiah or Elijah or Amos. He appears lean, ascetical, given to fasting and never drinking wine; he is a voice crying out from the desert wilderness, one who lives at the margins of the social world. Jesus, on the other hand, travels the villages and towns and is immersed in the daily life of people. He is frequently found eating and drinking, so much so that some accused him of being a glutton and a drunkard, not to mention being a table companion of public sinners (Luke 7:33-34)! John would never have occasioned such scandal. The root of differences like these had to lie in contrasting conceptions of who God was, what God wanted, and what the kingdom of God meant. Indeed, Jesus must have read and appropriated the Scriptures his own way, in terms of his own experience of the God whom he knew as Father.

One needs to keep in mind, therefore, that there is no single, uniform view or notion of God which runs through the whole of the Old Testament. Besides, the typical reader would most likely not be overly impressed with the way God frequently appears there. Indeed, if it were not for the fact that God is portrayed differently, say, in the Book of Exodus or Deuteronomy than in the prophetic Books of Isaiah, Amos, or Hosea, it would be impossible to read the scriptural texts selectively. There would be no selection available, no alternative texts to choose from. Nor would there be any imaginative room or distance between ideas and experiences to allow someone like Jesus to relate to God in a creatively new way. In that case, Jesus' view of God would have been absolutely discontinuous with Jewish Scriptures. The so-called God of the Old Testament would have been the God of the nation of Israel pure and simple, with all the narrow regionalism which that implies. In short, the experience of God among the patriarchs differs from that of the prophets, except that for both patriarchs and prophets the God of Israel is a God who acts in history and has proven himself faithful to his promises.

As we think about God, then, we find ourselves appealing to passages from various parts of Scripture, leaning more heavily on some texts than on others. Whenever the Christian reads the Old Testament, he or she does so as a *Christian reader*. That is to say, the Christian brings his or her own Christian faith to the ancient Jewish texts which make up the Hebrew Scriptures or Old Testament. Throughout this chapter, as we reflected on the implications of the creation story in the Book of Genesis, we also had to draw on other portions of Scripture in order to catch sight of the fuller range of God's promise or commitment to creation. In fact, for a Christian, the story of creation would be incomplete unless it included an account of the resurrection of Jesus.

Chapter Two

Resurrection as Promise

The central Christian belief is the resurrection of Jesus. Because Jesus was raised from the dead, there is a story to tell about him. Without Easter, there would have been no gospels, no Church or sacraments, and no uniquely Christian experience of God. "If Christ has not been raised," Paul concludes, "your faith is vain" (1 Cor 15:17). When the evangelists began composing their narratives about Jesus, they already knew the outcome of the story. Resurrection faith filled their minds from the first stroke of their pens. What the resurrection actually meant, however, is not all that easy to explain. No doubt, in raising Jesus from the dead God had demonstrated conclusively that there was an afterlife; but proof of the existence of the afterlife was not the primary meaning of the resurrection. Many people already believed in it, although for most people of Jesus' day the resurrection of the dead would not take place until the end of history. Jesus' resurrection had occurred in the middle of history, which suggested to some that the final age of the world had dawned.

Nor would it be enough to say that in raising Jesus from the dead, God had authenticated the divine nature of Jesus. Again, it is true that the resurrection set in motion a process of reflection in that direction. Early on, the Church had concluded that, by raising Jesus up, the Father had exalted him to his own right hand and made him Lord (Acts 2:36). Within a few centuries, that process would take a philosophical turn and identify Jesus, the Son ("being son" at first understood in biblical terms), with the Son of God and second Person of the Trinity ("being son" framed now in metaphysical terms). But the resurrection did not dictate that the reflective process had to move along those lines, for the

Church also came to believe that all of us would likewise be raised from the dead. Yet our resurrections would not be automatic confirmations of our possessing divine natures, unless, of course, we want to say that all of God's daughters and sons are destined to be raised from the dead; or rather, that none of us will reach our full stature as children of God until we, like Jesus, have been raised from the dead as well. The resurrection, in other words, is not, in and of itself, proof of the divinity of Jesus. "For just as in Adam all die," Paul writes, "so too in Christ shall all be brought to life, but each one in proper order: Christ the firstfruits; then, at his coming, those who belong to Christ" (1 Cor 15:22-23).

Some people interpret the resurrection as God's confirmation of the life and teaching of Jesus. In raising Jesus, God has indicated, once and for all, the divine preference for the poor, the outcast, and the powerless people of this world. The resurrection, according to this view, cannot be appreciated apart from the history which preceded it. For the resurrection is not simply the personal victory of one man, but it is the triumph of a man who was revealing to us how God wanted us to live, what God stood for, and what God was really like. Jesus' struggle against principalities and powers — against every form of injustice, oppression, and sin — was vindicated through the resurrection. Easter confirmed the divine option disclosed by some of the prophetic literature of Israel, namely, God's preferential love for the poor.

EASTER: THE EIGHTH DAY OF CREATION

Closer to our purposes here, however, lies another way to regard the resurrection, and that is as the work, so to speak, of the eighth day of creation. The resurrection completes our understanding of the meaning of creation itself. God creates in order to bring things to life, for our God is a God of the living, not of the dead (Matt 22:32). While the reality of death as the cessation of our lives on earth can hardly be denied (or reversed), the full scope of what life is cannot be grasped apart from the resurrection of Jesus. For what is life? Certainly, it is more than sheer physical existence. It is more than material, emotional, and social survival: "For life is more than food and the body more than clothing" (Luke 12:23). Full human life has to do with the Spirit, with freedom, with the capacity to serve and to forgive, to believe and to love. Life, we might say, is the uninterrupted possession of the Spirit, an abiding union with God, the one who created the heavens and the earth. Life is the ongoing, unbroken disposition to love, freely and selflessly. It is not acquired without struggle and suffering, which accounts for why (at least for Christians) the mystery of life and love is forever tied up with a mysticism of the Cross. Human beings are not fully created and alive until they are united with God; divine love, therefore, would fall short if it stopped just at the threshold of our becoming one in love with the God whose inner life is profoundly and everlastingly Love itself (1 John 4:8).

The resurrection constantly calls our attention to the divine creative purpose. In doing so, it becomes the principal Christian symbol of creation and divine promise. If the substance of that promise is God's faithfulness to creation, then the raising of Jesus testifies to divine fidelity. God will not allow his holy ones to undergo corruption (Ps 16:10; Acts 2:24ff). God has taken the side of life — not only life as opposed to the grave, but life as opposed to everything which here and now oppresses the human spirit. From his or her faith in Jesus risen, there emerges for the Christian a death-resistant confidence that ultimately the victory over every form of inhumanity will belong to people who are of God. Thus, men and women of Easter faith, confronted by death in any of the life-threatening forms it can assume — sickness, old age, violence, slavery and oppression, betrayal, and despair — find the courage to face it squarely and to pursue patiently works of justice, love, and peace. Resurrection faith pertains to life in this world. God, we believe, never abandons those whose first loyalty is to him.

Our personal experience of God's faithfulness and our ability to see the resurrection as the fulfillment of God's creative promise presuppose that we have contemplated and made our own the truth of creation. In other words, the possibility of experiencing divine faithfulness rests upon the realization that we are creatures and that we are still in the process of being formed. It also depends upon our having studied the created world with our hearts and discovered its goodness. Apart from this experience, all rhetoric about creation and resurrection is merely words. If theology courses had a laboratory component, as many science courses do, it would consist of prayer and spiritual direction; for the doctrine (and the mystery) of creation is not something merely to be researched and talked about. It needs to be contemplated and made one's own. We know God's faithfulness from within the experience of being created and being placed in a world God found to be good. A person's awareness of divine faithfulness is tied up with the experience of being grateful for the gift of life.

DIVINE FIDELITY AND RESURRECTION FAITH

There are undoubtedly other ways in which to regard the resurrection, too. One might begin trying to understand it through a sustained meditation on the present experience of Christians, for if Jesus has truly been raised from the dead, then our experience of God here and now will be affected by that fact. And this is what some readers see has taken place in the Gospel of John. Throughout the Fourth Gospel, it is the risen Jesus who teaches, heals, and encounters people. The Gospel could even be viewed as a prolonged meditation on life in the Spirit, that is, as living in communion with the risen Lord. As such, the Fourth Gospel instructs us about how we, too, might relate to the Jesus who, as the living Lord, abides in our midst, guiding us, sustaining us with new life, and tying us deeply into the mystery of God's love.

This perspective on the resurrection is profoundly rich. There is a particular perception of divine fidelity which is to be experienced only within the horizon of resurrection faith, and the point of departure here is not so much the Gospel of John as an insight of St. Paul. For Paul, perhaps more than any other New Testament writer, expressed the mystery of the disciple's being joined to Jesus in his dying and rising. In fact, the key to reading and appreciating the content of Paul's letters is to keep recalling that nearly everything Paul says proceeds from the vantage point of the resurrection. He writes: "We were indeed buried with him through baptism into death, so that, just as Christ was raised from the dead by the glory of the Father, we too might live in newness of life" (Rom 6:4). This newness of life of which Paul speaks is something which has already begun for those who have been united to Christ Jesus. New life is the consequence of having died with Jesus. Paul continues: "We know that Christ, raised from the dead, dies no more; death no longer has power over him. As to his death, he died to sin once and for all; as to his life, he lives for God. *Consequently, you too must think of yourselves as [being] dead to sin and living for God in Christ Jesus"* (6:9-11). And later he says: "But you are not in the flesh; on the contrary, you are in the spirit, if only the Spirit of God dwells in you. . . . But if Christ is in you, although the body is dead because of sin, the spirit is alive because of righteousness" (8:9-10).

Paul plays on the terms "life" and "death." While he undoubtedly has his eye on our physical death and future life with God, he is also assuring us that life and death are things to be experienced even now. The body of sin dies, crucified with Jesus (Gal 2:19-20), but the human spirit lives in newness of life. Through our dying and rising with Jesus, we discover a way of living which would otherwise have been impossible for us. There is a brand new way to live, but that way does not become accessible until we have died, not physically but inwardly. I think that this is what Jesus meant when he said that those who lose their lives for his sake will find them (Mark 8:35). And there is a special experience of divine faithfulness associated with this newness of life. But what is it?

To begin, we need to reflect on what it means to die with Jesus, or as the Gospel text puts it, to lose one's life for Jesus' sake. Sooner or later, each of us has to come to terms with the certain prospect of his or her own death. For Christians, however, death should no longer have any power; God, in Jesus, has broken its dominion over us. This belief does not lead us to deny the reality of having to die, nor make us oblivious to the suffering and diminishment which often accompany the process of dying. But we do not believe in death; we believe in life. Dying is the final stage in our being created; we are not being created for death, but for life.

The follower of Jesus knows what it is to die ahead of time, as it were. Day by day, there is a slow dying to self which inevitably accompanies our being with Jesus, our taking up the Cross daily and following him. Most of the time, this daily dying is undramatic. It consists of the hundreds of moments when we are called upon to prefer others to ourselves, to take their interests into account. Parents are perhaps the clearest examples of this. Mothers and fathers automatically come to think first of their children: learning to change their plans at a moment's notice, not buying something for themselves because they need instead to provide for their families, disciplining themselves for the sake of giving the best example possible to their daughters and sons, acquiring patience, at times suffering keen disappointment, worrying, attending to emergencies, coping with adolescent growing pains, and so forth. There is a special kind of asceticism which is called forth from us in our efforts to be Christian parents.

In addition to this, however, there is another form of dying ahead of time, and that is the wholesale inversion of values which comes from making a fundamental option for the kingdom of God. The language may sound large and abstract, but the reality is quite simple. Over a period of time, as a result of continual exposure to the story of Jesus, one begins to think with him, to live with him, to see the world through the eyes of the gospel. The teaching, parables, and example of Jesus become the lens through which one looks at life. Through prayerful, imaginative immersion in the story of Jesus, a person puts on, as it were, the mind and heart of Jesus, as when Paul writes, "Have among yourselves the same attitude that is also yours in Christ Jesus" (Phil 2:5), or "But we have the mind of Christ" (1 Cor 2:16), or "For all of you who were baptized into Christ have clothed yourselves with Christ" (Gal 3:27).

The result of this daily being-with-Jesus through prayer and imagination is conversion: an inversion of values and outlook so thorough and radical that one has in effect died to everything which does not conform to the gospel. Such a person, even without being conscious of it, is ready to do whatever may be necessary, whatever circumstances call for, in the process of following Jesus. Even the prospect of having to lay down one's life, literally, for the sake of Jesus (or for the sake of those for whom he lived and died) is no longer frightening. One lives with that possibility continually. Such people are truly free, truly poor in spirit, for they have in a penetrating way already died. The life they now live they live for God in Christ Jesus. This is the kind of life, I believe, which Paul had in mind when he spoke of our being

joined with Jesus in his death and rising with him to newness of
life. This experience of living in the world as if one had already
died to its false values, its hollow promises, and its sinful seduc-
tions is the spiritual prerequisite for understanding the meaning of
divine faithfulness. The person who has died with Jesus has become liberated from the power and dominion of death.

What, then, do people who have died with Jesus know about
divine faithfulness that the rest of us have not yet learned? First of
all, they have learned that there is life after death. Like swimmers
who have taken a plunge into deep waters and risen again to the
surface, they have learned that the waters could not hold them
down. Yet no matter how much they describe their experience to
the rest of us and reassure us as we contemplate making the same
plunge, there is no way we shall discover the truth until we, like
them, have let go of the securities to which we cling.

Perhaps, however, the experience is not so much that of letting
go as one of realizing, after passing much of one's life in Jesus'
company, that one's life has been radically, and probably irreversibly, changed. One looks back one day at the landscape and realizes what until then was only known dimly, or maybe even
unconsciously: that one has indeed traveled a great distance — so
far, in fact, that there is no going back. Like Abraham, one left
the home and land of one's parents and journeyed to a new land,
the "land flowing with milk and honey" (Exod 3:8). "The Lord
said to Abram: 'Go forth from the land of your kinsfolk and from
your father's house to a land that I will show you'" (Gen 12:1).
The land which God shows is a land of promise. It always lies
ahead of us; it can be neither envisioned nor reached without
faith and trust. For the people of Israel, the land was an actual
place in the ancient Near East. For the Church, however, the
"land" has a symbolic meaning. The image of Abraham's journeying is religiously rich and suggestive of every believer's condition
in this world. For Abraham, as for us, there was no going back
once he had encountered the living God. The firm determination
to continue one's journey despite all obstacles and setbacks testifies to the depth of that encounter. Even more, it testifies to a person's daily experience of the firmness of God's grace: the grace
which keeps confirming our holy, lifegiving desires.

While the journey of faith, in retrospect, might appear to have been rather unremarkable (because foundational change in the human soul occurs silently and gradually), the consequence is dramatic. Just as the extraordinary, surprising harvest of the gospel parable defies any ordinary farmer's wildest expectations (Matt 13:8), the liberated humanity of those who have died with Jesus stretches our capacity to believe that such a new way of living is actually possible. The ones who have journeyed with Jesus acquire that unshakable confidence in the power, the justice, and the goodness of God which can only be known by someone who has been raised from the dead. Divine faithfulness is never more clear or comprehensible. To the rest of us, still clinging to the conditions of the present age, their way of thinking and acting could even appear as so much nonsense. Those who have been living with Jesus seem to have taken flight from reality and leave of their senses; their living has become embarrassingly impractical, for sheer physical existence is no longer the highest good. Since they have already died with Jesus, they would be willing to surrender everything the present age could offer in terms of comfort, security, and recognition. Not that their attention is fastened naively and prematurely upon eternal life in heaven. On the contrary, as a result of having died with Jesus, they have risen to newness of life in this world, witnessing to the presence of the kingdom of God and to God's desire that the present age be totally transformed. For what God, as the Creator of life, wants for this world is its blessedness: justice, peace, and communion. Just as it can be said that the crucified Jesus rose to new life in his disciples (he had promised not to abandon his own), so too it might be said that the followers of Jesus who lay down their life rise to new life in the community of believers.

If the risen Jesus were not alive in us, then Paul's great insight into the meaning of the resurrection (not to mention the insight which guided the writing of the Fourth Gospel) would utterly collapse. There would be no Church, no people of God, no body of Christ, no community of disciples. By the same token, why should we not be able to say that the spirit of the saints rises up within the hearts and souls of the people of God, prompting them to do and to dare great things with the same sort of passionate commitment to the kingdom? This, I believe, is the meaning of Archbishop Romero's beautiful, poignant words spoken shortly before his death: "I have often been threatened with death. I must tell you, as a Christian, I do not believe in death without resurrection. If I am killed, I shall rise in the Salvadoran people. I say so without boasting, with the greatest humility."

Divine faithfulness proves itself, finally, in the experience of those who have been united with Jesus in his dying and rising. Confident of God's power to create for life, they are prepared to risk everything, should circumstances force them to, for the sake of their brothers and sisters. Again, perhaps, this helps to explain why Paul could write: "Therefore, I am content with weaknesses, insults, hardships, persecutions, and constraints, for the sake of Christ; for when I am weak, then I am strong" (2 Cor 12:10). "Power made perfect in weakness" is one of Paul's great resurrection formulas, illumining, as it does, the apostle's *experience* of being with Jesus. It was precisely in his moments of weakness and powerlessness that Paul experienced the strength and power of the risen Christ. Moreover, this experience is public; other men and women can verify it for themselves. They, like Paul, can catch the fidelity of God to creation from the other side of death, provided, of course, they stand there with Jesus.

THE STORY OF JESUS: LIVING A LIBERATED EXISTENCE

In a sense, it might be said that Jesus was living a resurrected existence even before Easter, for he had already "died" to the present age. The Cross marked not just the historical outcome and consequence of his ministry, but the very process leading up to it. Jesus had already discovered that confidence in God which enabled him to accept the Cross when it finally came. For the gospel reader, this is what helps to make sense of Jesus' predictions about his approaching suffering and death. Whatever the historical basis of those predictions might be, the fact is that Jesus was already disposed to accept the fate of the rejected prophet. He was already prepared to suffer the consequence of speaking God's word boldly and faithfully. The Cross, in other words, was on the scene long before the final days of Jesus' life.

Where did Jesus achieve mastery over death? At what point had its dominion been broken for him? Again, taking the gospel story on its own terms, such a moment might have occurred in the desert when Jesus struggled with Satan, for it was in the wilderness, before his public ministry began, that he had to contend with the obstacles and stumbling blocks (the "satans") which would have prevented him from being faithful to his mission. Jesus died to riches, to honor and recognition, to the desire for power and control over others, to presumed prerogatives (as if the hardness of his mission would automatically entitle him to a unique status before God). In the desert, Jesus died to himself.

The result of Jesus' dying in the wilderness was, first and foremost, his being able to see the concerns of God with the utmost clarity. The kingdom counted above all else. For its sake, a person would abandon everything; he would sell every single possession in order to obtain it (Matt 13:44-47). By dying to everything else, Jesus was able to view reality in terms of what mattered most. Scripture had commanded that we love the Lord absolutely and unconditionally: "Hear, O Israel! The Lord is our God, the Lord alone! Therefore, you shall love the Lord, your God, with all your heart, and with all your soul, and with all your strength" (Deut 6:4-5). What mattered most, then, was unswerving love and obedience to God — to the Lord who had created the heavens and the earth, who had called Abraham and formed a people after his own heart, whose creative care extended to all the peoples of the earth, and whose preferential love fell upon the poor and the oppressed.

The second result of Jesus' dying in the desert was a penetrating, radicalizing freedom. God liberated Jesus, too; otherwise, how could Jesus have identified with the condition of his people? How would he have related to the story of God's rescuing the people of Israel from slavery, an event which the Scriptures brought before the people's minds constantly? How could he bypass an experience of the liberating power of God, especially he whose ministry consisted so much in setting others free — free from sickness, free from sin and guilt, free from fear? But one might wonder from what Jesus needed to be liberated.

To answer this question, one has to look back to the temptation episode. If there had been no real temptation, there would have been no real need for liberation either. Living totally for God may not have come any more easily to Jesus than it does to the rest of us. Had Jesus been timid, wondering whether he could take up the prophetic mantle after John the Baptist was imprisoned? Had he been attracted to a more directly militant role in bringing about political and social change? He was certainly very much aware of all the injustice and misfortune around him; but how would he change it? Should he take advantage of the support of the crowds? Was there some subtle danger, as he set about announcing the kingdom, that he might let himself stand at the center of things instead of God?

Such questions are little more than imaginative guesses, yet they may shed some light on the process of Jesus' own liberation. If he was truly tempted; if he truly stood as a creature before his Creator, with all the dependency which this implies; if he, like the rest of us, lived within a daily process of being made (for God's creative power is steadily at work in our lives); if Jesus was at all sensitive to the concrete, historical needs of his people and if he was at all touched by the message of John the Baptist; if he shared the resentment of his countrymen at their land being occupied by a ruthless foreign power; if he felt indignant and angry over the injustice he saw about him and compassion for those at the bottom of society; if he had identified in any way with the concerns of Israel's prophets such as Amos, Hosea, Micah, and Isaiah (otherwise, why would some of his countrymen have thought that Jesus was one of the prophets of old come back to life?); in short, if Jesus was fully and truly a human being whose life was shaped by being born at a particular time and place; then one could reasonably speak of his being liberated, too, precisely so that, once liberated, he could lead his sisters and brothers to the same freedom.

In Jesus' life, as in ours, the mystery of divine grace and human response held sway. In his life, as in ours, everything depended upon his answering God freely and unreservedly. His temptations, then, were real; his struggle with conflicting spirits was no fiction. In renouncing Satan, he "died" to self; but in dying to self, he came radically alive for God. Henceforth, he would live without fear, for he was free; and being free of fear, he had nothing to lose: neither riches nor reputation nor the trappings of success nor life itself. They were already gone.

The freedom which Jesus won penetrated to the core of his soul. From there it would shape every aspect of his being and his mission; in one way or another, that freedom seems to appear on nearly every page of the gospel story. Jesus was free to be for others. He was free to be among those who were downtrodden and living from hand to mouth at the edges of society. He was free to keep the company of sinful men and women, many of whom would have been politically and socially expendable, and even to number them among his friends. Jesus was free to confront well-connected people, to risk their hostility and anger, and to face the prospect of persecution and death. In all of this, Jesus lived out of his experience of divine faithfulness. Were this not so, he would not have been able, honestly and convincingly, to call other people to believe. If Jesus had not personally experienced God's faithfulness, then what point would there have been in proclaiming, "This is the time of fulfillment" (Mark 1:15), or having read from the scroll of the prophet Isaiah, "Today this scripture passage is fulfilled in your hearing" (Luke 4:21)? On what basis could he have made such claims, unless he had truly found God to be faithful to his word? Jesus did not merely announce a message which had been mysteriously communicated to him. He preached what he believed, and he believed because he had experienced God's faithfulness and love.

The desert experience proved to Jesus that God would not abandon him, or anyone else for that matter, in a moment of spiritual crisis. We have to believe that Jesus was a man of faith prior to his going into the wilderness. It was faith, after all, which brought him to the Jordan to listen to the preaching of John the Baptist and to receive the baptism of repentance as so many of his countrymen were doing. And it was the call of the Spirit which drove him to the wilderness — not purely for the sake of undergoing temptation, but rather, we should imagine, to wrestle with the conflicting voices or spirits which he faced regarding his future, to pray and to think about how he ought to respond to the grace which had come over him so powerfully at his baptism. The desert had become the preferred haunt of those seeking God's will, the place where they could purify their hearts, sort out their intentions and desires, and learn how to listen to the word of God which was so mysteriously revealed in the silence and stillness of the wilderness.

The practice of seeking out a desolate place to meet God in solitude remained with Jesus all his life (Mark 1:35, 6:46; John 6:15). Jesus entered the desert as a believer, probably not knowing what would transpire there among the barren wastes, the scorching heat by day and the freezing cold by night, and the wild beasts. As a result, God would have to show him that when a person of faith takes such a risk in order to examine the desires and fears lying in the depths of his soul for the sake of discovering what God might be asking of him, God would not desert him. Even through the darkest nights of his searching and struggling, God would be there to strengthen and illumine him, and to confirm his hope. Jesus would have made his own the experience of the Psalmist:

"Where can I go from your spirit?
  from your presence where can I flee?
For you darkness itself is not dark,
  and night shines as the day."
(Ps 139:7, 12)

WHAT THIS MEANS FOR US

The point of the reflection we have been making is this. By creating us, God has made us a promise: God has promised to bring us to life. For God to create without pledging to remain faithful to creation would contradict the Christian idea and experience of God as Creator. That promise is underscored and reaffirmed, it is illumined and opened up from within, so to speak, in the raising of Jesus from the dead. God's faithfulness to the divine promise to bring us to the fullness of life is proven by the Spirit's enabling us to lead a resurrected existence. We, too, are called to live as men and women who have already died. From this, several things follow.

The ethical attitude of the kingdom is radical. (Jesus' teaching about love and forgiveness, about riches and material possessions, and the practical conclusions to be drawn from his parables about what God is like, all presuppose that we are living a risen existence.) Without the experience of being joined to Jesus in his dying and rising, and the consequent reconfiguring of the way we believe, hope, and love, Christianity is reduced to a religion of ethical principles and commands which most people will find extremely difficult to practice faithfully. The message of Jesus — the ethical attitude of the kingdom — depends upon what an earlier age called the supernatural outlook: the Easter Christian lives on a supernatural plane. Only on that plane does the message of Jesus make full sense; only by sharing in the life of the risen Jesus can his words and example be put into practice. The manner of living required by the gospel is both unintelligible and impractical (at least according to the standards of the present age) apart from the Easter mystery.

But proper moral behavior is not really the heart of the matter here. The central issue is our experience of divine faithfulness: the steady presence of God which makes us *want* to live a resurrected existence here and now, and strengthens us as we try. Many Christians discover the meaning of faithfulness in someone's commitment to them in a marriage relationship or in a close friendship. There they find the motivation to live out a gospel ideal and learn about the merit of struggling to make a relationship work. There, too, they acquire their conviction about the wonder and the worth of human life. For men and women of faith, the hidden ground of all human relationships is the grace and faithfulness of God. Those who fight to stay alive, not so much physically as humanly and spiritually; who resist all the forces that would grind away their hope and holiest resolutions; who refuse to renounce their belief in the goodness of creation and the giftedness of life, no matter how bleak their lives become; or who have found the courage to take a risk (even when things turn out quite differently from what they had hoped or expected): such people as these have known the faithfulness of God.

Even in Jesus' case, things turned out otherwise than what he had expected. He had preached the imminent arrival of the kingdom of God, caught up, no doubt, in the apocalyptic enthusiasm shared by many people of his time. But that is not what hap-

pened. The kingdom did not come in the way Jesus had an-
nounced. Instead, God raised Jesus from the dead and thereby
inaugurated something new within human history. The same will
have to be true for us. God will not permit our holiest desires and
efforts to lie barren in the earth. From them and through them,
the creative power and love of God continue to work in the
world, forming its history and drawing it to fulfillment. The sound
of divine promise will echo throughout the universe: ''Behold, I
make all things new'' (Rev 21:5).

Chapter Three

The Church as Sign of God's Promise

One of the keenest conceptual setbacks which the early Church faced was the delay of the second coming of Jesus. Jesus believed that the kingdom would arrive soon; such was the mentality of many people of his day, including John the Baptist. In his own life, as a result of his rejection by his own people and his impending death, Jesus doubtlessly had to face an enormous reversal in his thinking about what exactly God's plan for him and for Israel was. Perhaps he and his disciples believed that, even if he had to suffer first, the kingdom would still be right around the corner. With his death, God somehow would usher in the kingdom, a brand new reality which would spell liberation, justice, and peace for the people of Israel.

Paul, too, shared that outlook. Filled with enthusiasm as he set about preaching his gospel, Paul figured that the consummation of all things was close at hand. He was able to account for the delay of Jesus' reappearance by reasoning to himself that, first, the Gentiles had to hear the good news. Only then, when the full complement of the Gentiles had been grafted onto the people of God, would his own Jewish race finally accept the word about Jesus, and only then would the messianic age be inaugurated (Rom 11:25). Such was Paul's fervent hope. In time, succeeding generations would have to adjust their theology and their mission to the fact that the delay was turning out to be much longer than anyone in the first generation of believers had anticipated. One of the results of this conceptual adjustment was the emergence of a theology of the Church which took into account that God's redemptive plan for the human race would continue as long as the human race survived. This long-range view was certainly advantageous to the Gentiles, who discovered in the Church's life and message an experience of community and salvation. It was not helpful to the Jewish people, however, because for them it appeared that God had hedged on the promise to liberate and redeem God's chosen people, a promise that should not have to wait until the end of time for its fulfillment.

Israel never got the savior it was looking for. Or rather, the great social, economic and political change which was so eagerly anticipated (for what else could an oppressed people reasonably want in this life?) failed to arrive. The disciples of Jesus had to accommodate their own thinking about the future to this fact. In the meantime, the message of Jesus was being preached with increasing success among the Gentiles. For them, the imminent transformation of Israel, so much at the heart of Jesus' proclamation about the kingdom, did not matter as much. The Gentiles welcomed and accepted the gospel message, even though the Jewish people themselves had reason to be disillusioned because the great promises of God, which they might have hoped were soon to be fulfilled through the prophet Jesus (since his miracles and teaching would have stirred those hopes), remained unrealized.

In recalling this history, one cannot escape observing how the cherished hopes of many people were not fulfilled, which must have left them disappointed and confused. Individuals who felt themselves close to God could still be mistaken on a matter of what appeared to them to be of fundamental importance, namely, the imminent arrival of God's reign in the world. One would like to think that John the Baptist, since he was the last of the great prophets, would have been told as much. One would expect that Jesus, whose faith and teaching would become the foundation of a great religion, would have known as much. And certainly, if the risen Jesus had discovered anything, he would surely have learned that God's plans were quite different from what he had envisioned while on earth. Why, then, as part of his resurrection appearances and why, indeed, in his self-revelation to the apostle Paul did the risen Jesus not correct this misapprehension about the endtime?

One would have to conclude that communicating correct information was not an essential part of the Easter appearances or of the work of the risen Jesus, and that the matters of the timing of the kingdom's arrival and Jesus' return in glory were not all that important in God's eyes. Yet one sobering fact remains: Hopes were not realized in the way that people had imagined they would be. By giving those hopes a "spiritual" interpretation, that is, by displacing them from concrete changes in this world and reviewing them as referring primarily to interior change, moral renewal, and the formation of a spiritual community whose major task was to conduct people through this life to the next, the early Church may have rescued the life of Jesus from oblivion and explained (or theologized) away the scandal of unrealized prophecy.

Yet, what lesson do we draw from the fact that things did not eventuate as Jesus seems to have believed they would? What are we to think about the fact that John the Baptist and Paul were likewise mistaken? Or perhaps to put the question in a way that is more helpful to us as we endeavor to remain men and women of faith, in the end did Jesus have to reconcile himself to being disappointed, even disillusioned with God? Did Paul? While we may take some initial consolation in the fact that Jesus, like so many human beings, experienced a collapse of hope or vision that almost bordered on feeling totally abandoned by God (Mark 15:34), sooner or later we have to face the desolation of not comprehending why God permits such things to happen.

GOD AND THE PROBLEM OF COLLAPSED EXPECTATIONS

The experience of feeling let down by God is not new. It occurs whenever people's hopes have been raised as a result, say, of their reading and taking seriously the gospel, or of being moved to the point of conversion by the genuine holiness of other human beings, only to discover that the rest of the world has not changed but continues to crawl along its sinful, timid path. It is hard to explain why, exactly, hope becomes aroused. Part of the reason may be an individual's temperament or disposition. Some people are inclined to dream more than others, to want more out of life by giving more of themselves. During some part of their lives, they may embark upon a vision quest, responding to a call lying deep within their souls which sets them searching for their life's grand plan. They feel a need to affirm their lives (or to be affirmed by

Life itself) by becoming important to history, that is, by making a difference within the lives of other men and women. Fired by a conviction that their times are special, and impelled by a belief that the Spirit has opened a window of fresh possibility, they want to collaborate with the Holy. Since God alone can guarantee the lasting meaningfulness of things, whoever works with God necessarily is involved in something of permanent, even of transcendental value. The notion of mission — of being personally sent by God — is richly attractive; indeed, it is almost romantic.

Others might simply have awakened to the realities around them. An event or experience of some sort turns on a kind of cosmic switch in their hearts. Perhaps for the first time they feel the need to figure things out, to develop a lifestyle or a mission which enables them to respond to the demand (or to the call) which reality has thrust upon them. It may not have been a vision quest or some mystical intuition about what truly counts in life that prompted them, but simply a concrete encounter with someone in dire need of another human being's help. Perhaps the person was overwhelmed by the poverty or the injustice or the misery which another person or group was suffering. One thinks of Mother Teresa's encounter with the impoverished people of Calcutta who were literally dying outside the gate of the convent school where she had been teaching, or Archbishop Oscar Romero's inner awakening to the diabolical nature of the injustice in Salvadoran society as a result of the assassination of one of his socially involved priests. Or maybe one recalls the classic conversion story of the Apostle Paul himself. Having fallen to the ground in an encounter with the risen Jesus, Paul discovered him as the one who now suffers in his sisters and brothers: "Saul, Saul, why are you persecuting me?" (Acts 9:4).

In each case, people already believers made an internal about-face. God opened them to a brand new way of envisioning the divine relationship with people — among the dying, among the oppressed, among the persecuted. As a result, their lives were redirected according to a mission they sensed that God had entrusted to them, a mission which they would probably not have embraced unless they also believed and hoped that they would be cooperating with the Spirit itself. In other words, they grasped, perhaps at a level that went beyond all reasoning, the rightness of what they were going to have to do. Indeed, the details of their respective missions had to unfold day by day, as they continued responding in faith to their inner awakening. But it would be next to impossible to imagine their having ventured anything at all unless they had been profoundly moved by hope, by joy, and by a sense of God's closeness. Where else would they have acquired their passion?

Whatever the particular reason behind their awakening, the fact is that human beings can become contaminated by hope. The fact is, too, that God is usually at the bottom of such infection. Unfortunately, enthusiasm and inspiration can be diluted and undone by the inertia of the world's sinfulness. One thinks, for example, of those for whom the Second Vatican Council spelled an experience of great freedom and freshness. Their inner senses awoke to the possibility that the Church truly is a Church of the Spirit and that Christianity, which for many had grown lifeless, uninspiring, and out of touch with the realities of this world, was actually a manifestation of the Spirit after all. The Council shook many things up, but above all it aroused hope and enthusiasm, which dared people to trust in the power of the Spirit to make all things new.

The changes which the Council initiated, but even more importantly, the attitude of freedom, of hope, and of appreciation for the world and human culture which it demonstrated, captured the imaginations of many and rekindled their traditional loyalties. Being a Christian, the Council seemed to say, made exquisite sense in a world which sorely needed what the Church and the gospel were able to give it, namely, a sense of direction, a conviction about God's abiding presence among us, and a willingness both to listen and to learn, especially to listen to and learn from the voices of the poor and powerless whose lives clamored for justice and for full human liberation.

The Council quickened many hearts. Yet now, nearly thirty years later, a good number of people find themselves wondering what happened to that Spirit and what has become of the Church. For in recent years, the Church appears to have moved backwards, almost as if resentful, even angry, that so much spirit and hope had been released. The Church has retrenched. Perhaps nervous about the children of God inheriting the full measure of the Spirit and freedom which had been promised to them, the Church appears to be deliberately deflating the hopes of those who have been praying that the effect of the Council will continue well into the next century. It is not necessary to rehearse here all the reasons for this regression. The point is simply that the experience of many people today of the Church or religion or of faith itself, is one of being disillusioned and disheartened. Was the Council truly an event of the Spirit after all? Did God re-awaken us to an ancient possibility, only to let us down in the end?

The experience of the Council is but one example. From time to time, an individual or a group takes the promises of God with the utmost seriousness, as Jesus did. He heard the great prophetic texts, meditated on them, and believed them: Jesus took God seriously. Many people since then have taken God in Jesus with the same earnestness. They have been excited by him and his message, and have attempted, in the midst of the ordinariness of life, to keep their faith vision alive and to pass it along to the next generation.

Charismatic energy and confidence are hard to maintain, however. The Spirit prompts an individual to do or to dare something, and in the prompting or inspirational stage, there is usually a great deal of animated discussion, sharing, and enthusiastic action. But as the activity increases and as time marches along, the animating vision is increasingly internalized and made one's own. Those coming on the scene at a later moment normally have not shared the foundational experience. The doing and the thinking then become more routine; the founding inspiration can be covered over in the very effort to preserve and transmit it. That is why individuals, communities, and important human relationships such as friendships and marriages need continually to be scrutinized and renewed. That is also why the Church, if it is to be spiritually vigorous, needs to keep recalling and celebrating the prospects, attitudes, and directions created by the great Council of our time. Indeed, it needs ever to be recovering its roots in the first Pentecost.

According to Mark's version of the gospel story, Jesus began his public ministry with the proclamation, "This is the time of fulfillment. The kingdom of God is at hand. Repent, and believe in the gospel" (Mark 1:15). A few years later, on the road to Jerusalem, the disciples are asking who among them is the greatest and, presumably, most qualified to sit on either side of Jesus when he finally assumes power (Mark 9:33-34 and 10:35-37). When we come to the moment of the Ascension, we hear the disciples, who had responded to Jesus' initial proclamation by leaving their homes and livelihoods, asking, "Lord, are you at this time going to restore the kingdom to Israel?" (Acts 1:6). If there was a different meaning to Jesus' inaugural message than the restoration of justice throughout the land, the disciples, who had spent several years in Jesus' company, listening and learning, still did not comprehend it. Several years later, they were still waiting eagerly. At least for the disciples, Jesus' announcement about the kingdom's being at hand had not come true.

Once again, it may be instructive to recall the psalms. There, in some of the hymns of complaint, God is constantly being reminded of the divine promise to be faithful to the people of Israel. For God had said:

"I will not violate my covenant;
  the promise of my lips I will not alter.
Once, by my holiness, have I sworn:
  I will not be false to David.
His posterity shall continue forever,
  and his throne shall be like the sun before me;
Like the moon, which remains forever —
  a faithful witness in the sky."

But the Psalmist goes on to add:

Yet you have rejected and spurned
  and been enraged at your anointed.
You have renounced the covenant with your servant,
  and defiled his crown in the dust.
You have broken down all his walls;
  you have laid his stronghold in ruins.
(Ps 89:35-41)

As if this lapse of memory, or of fidelity, were not enough, the Psalmist also cries, in the face of another experience of national calamity:

All this has come upon us, though we have not
   forgotten you,
   nor have we been disloyal to your covenant;
Our hearts have not shrunk back,
   nor our steps turned aside from your path,
Though you have thrust us down into a place of misery
   and covered us over with darkness.
If we had forgotten the name of our God
   and stretched out our hands to a strange god,
Would not God have discovered this?
   For he knows the secrets of the heart.
(Ps 44:18-22)

Sometimes the psalms reflect Israel's rhythmic experience of sin, chastisement, repentance, and renewed blessing. Punishment is anticipated in the wake of Israel's failure to obey the divine word. At other times, however, misfortune strikes even though the people have been faithful to their side of the covenant. There does not appear to be any logic to God's activity in history. Similarly, one might be inclined to argue that the explanation for the kingdom's failure to arrive lies, at least in part, with human beings themselves: they simply have not repented and believed. The failure to believe, moreover, brings about its own chastisement. Humanity continues to labor under the heavy burden of sin and guilt which translates concretely into oppression, violence, injustice, hatred, and despair.

Yet this cannot be the entire picture, either. Some men and women do energetically and enthusiastically cooperate with God by responding to the gospel. They share Jesus' conviction that God will act decisively on behalf of those who seek the kingdom of God. Even then, however, God does not seem to deliver; God does not make good on the proclamation of the kingdom which Jesus preached. Instead, one encounters a constant struggle against the tides of complacency, fear, and outright disbelief, even on the part of those who claim to have accepted the gospel.

One could, of course, switch gospels and adopt the approach of John the evangelist's Jesus: "My kingdom does not belong to this world" (John 18:36). And in a sense, that is correct: Jesus' kingdom will never conform to the standards and attitudes of the present age. But if the kingdom were purely and simply other-worldly, then the Herods and Pilates of this world would never have anything to fear from those who continue to believe that with God all things are possible, even here and now.

The truth of the matter is, I believe, that we simply should not concede the objection that the kingdom has not come. What is at stake is how we wish to conceive the kingdom: as a towering reality like the mighty cedars of Lebanon, or as a lowly reality like the humble mustard shrub. Indeed, something has come as a result of Jesus' life, death, and resurrection. The problem is not with what God has failed to accomplish; rather, the problem is that we stand between a full vision and its partial realization in history. We stand between a future possibility that grabs hold of our desires and imaginations, and the often humble, unseen, ordinary yet mysterious transformation of human lives under the power of grace.

BECOMING VULNERABLE TO THE DIVINE: THE RISK OF OPENING ONESELF TO GOD

To open oneself to hearing and making one's own the divine promises is to become vulnerable. Indeed, vulnerability is an inevitable part of every close relationship since in a close relationship one begins to feel and to appreciate another person's desires, concerns, and experiences. At the core of the divine promise is God's faithfulness, as we have already seen. But promise also reveals desire: God wants to be faithful, and more. God also wants to bring us fully to life, which is another way of stating that there are divine desires for the world. For us, the clearest expression of divine desire for the human race is what Jesus preached, namely, the kingdom of God. To enter into a relationship with the living God, therefore, is to share God's desire for us, the divine plan in our regard.

But sharing that desire likewise entails becoming vulnerable, even as God in some mysterious way became vulnerable by creating us. For relationships not only expose us to another person's feelings. In relationships, we always run the risk of the other person's abandoning us or of not valuing the relationship as highly as we do. And this is the sort of thing which has made the unfolding of the divine creative plan so irregular and unsteady, at least as viewed from biblical eyes. The human response frequently fails to match God's desire on our behalf. The human race has not invested as much in its relationship with the Creator as the Creator has with us. In other words, the first one to suffer because a great plan or vision has not been realized is God. Such is the divine cost of dealing with creatures endowed with incompletely realized freedom.

Nevertheless, God is patient and everlastingly faithful. God is also everlastingly a visionary, who, as Scripture tells us, frequently visits men and women in their dreams. Just as none of us alone, by ourselves, can implement a vision for the benefit of other men and women (for we need their cooperation if the vision is going to take root and to spread); so too God, in a real sense, has to depend upon us to catch the fire. God, eternal Spirit, may also be everlastingly eager and charismatic, even unchangeably romantic.

Perhaps reflecting in this way will shed some light on the experience of disillusionment and disappointment which many men and women of faith have had to endure. We can be disappointed because things do not work out as we had hoped or expected, and this disappointment grows all the more intense the more we connected our hopes and plans with what we believed to be God's plan and inspiration. Sometimes, to be sure, we have simply miscalculated. Perhaps because our discernment did not proceed from true liberty of mind and affections, or perhaps because with the best of faith and intentions we were simply mistaken, we prematurely identified our plans with God's will. At other times, however, there may have been no miscalculation, no failure of interior liberty or concealed personal attachments. Something prompted by the Spirit still might not materialize because it has been blocked by human blindness or fear or laziness, or any of the other stumbling blocks by means of which good people are prevented from implementing their holy desires. In such cases, it is not God who has let us down, but other human beings. And viewing things from God's side, as it were, maybe this has been the major chord throughout humanity's relatively brief history on the earth. It is painful to share the divine experience of being abandoned by the very men and women for whom one wants everything which is good and holy.

THE CHURCH AS SIGN OF DIVINE FAITHFULNESS

The reflection we have been developing might seem to be a terribly lengthy introduction to the central idea of this chapter, but I believe these remarks provide the appropriate background for appreciating how the Church witnesses to God's fidelity. The Church was born, it would appear, amidst the collapsed expectations of the early generations of Christians. Yet the Church is not the fruit of disappointment and misunderstanding, but of intense energy, confidence, and newness of life. It is, and was meant to be, a compelling sign within human history of God's presence and abiding faithfulness. There is no doubt that all of us could list our complaints against the Church, and the more of its history we learn, the more criticisms we could level against it. In its authoritarianism and its periodic intolerance of spiritual freedom, new ways of thinking (especially in theology), and practically every manifestation of dissent, and by lending ideological legitimacy to some wretched abuses of human rights, the Church has frequently failed precisely in those areas where it ought to have set an example. Far too often the Church has succumbed to timidity and fear. In this way, at least, it has remained Petrine; Peter, too, in moments of crisis yielded to fear and cowardice.

But it would be extremely shortsighted to permit our attitude toward the Church to be dominated by its weaknesses. The Church, after all, remains the place where we heard the story of Jesus; it was in the Church that our faith was first planted and nurtured. The mystery of the Church is much larger than its institutional structure. Fundamentally, the Church in its truest and holiest dimension has been the community of Jesus' followers, the men and women who have striven throughout the centuries to give faithful witness to him by the way they lived out the gospel. Whenever the observer's eye gets distracted by the institution's ecclesiastical trappings, the flawed character of some of its official leaders, the record of its sinfulness, or its periodic addiction to traditionalism, we miss the most important reality; we overlook the faith and life-witness of those men and women who really follow Jesus, and who follow him as members of a community which, however imperfectly, continues to tell his story and proclaim his message. After all, no one person is more "Church" than another. All of us, together, are the people of God.

Sometimes the Church forgets the parables of Jesus. It begins to think and act as if it were the majestic cedar of Lebanon, rather than the humble mustard shrub. On such occasions the Spirit has to remind the Church, by raising up prophetic voices within it, of its origins in poverty and persecution. The believing community which formed in Jerusalem proclaimed the central mystery of faith: Jesus, the one whom the Father had raised from the dead, was the one rejected, humiliated, tortured, and abandoned. Jesus came to the Cross, moreover, precisely because he was undyingly faithful to the mission which God had entrusted to him. Jesus never abandoned God's concerns. Can the Church, then, ever expect to do or undergo anything less than what Jesus did and suffered? Can it ever expect to be more than the Church of the crucified One, with all that this implies?

The Church was not born as an afterthought. Rather, the only way for the mission and message of Jesus to reach into history was through a community of dedicated believers: men and women who had accepted the gospel, contemplated it, built their lives upon it, who would re-interpret it for different times and places and pass it along to their children and grandchildren. That community, like any organization of human beings, would have its own particular structure, customs, and teachings. But these social, public, or institutional aspects of the community as it developed and moved further along in history would always remain subordinate to the community's inner life and the Spirit from which that life came.

The Church, therefore, was not merely a social means for transmitting the gospel message across ages and cultures. Perhaps much more importantly, the Church was called into existence as a community which testified to the truthfulness of Jesus' message by the way it lived. And this is the area, of course, where failure is most likely to occur. Few can fault the Church's message. When scandal occurs, it generally results from the contradiction between practice and belief. For at least as far as the world is concerned, the principal proclamation about Jesus is less what Christians say about him and more how they live as a result of their baptismal profession of faith.

Although it is often the sinfulness of the Church that draws the quickest attention and criticism, there is another side to the Church's reality, namely, its holiness. People are often slower to notice this, since goodness is usually less fascinating than evil. Yet goodness (or holiness) is far more intriguing than sin. Sin is all too obvious; its presence in the Church provides many people with an excuse for not changing their lives by repenting and believing the gospel. Holiness — human wholeness — is much more attractive, however; it is a thing of beauty. The goodness of others entices us into wanting to be whole ourselves, into imitating those who have found freedom and grace, whose lives have been marked by the most profound love, gratitude, and liberty of heart.

Holiness is, of course, dramatically illustrated in the lives of. those whom the Church recognizes as saints; but it exists just as certainly, although less celebrated, in the lives of countless men and women whose manner of living is rather ordinary. They pray. They struggle to maintain their faith and courage from day to day in the midst of the numerous challenges and setbacks which ordinary human beings have to face. Trusting in the presence and providence of God, they endure the various forms of suffering that accompany the human condition: sickness; the diminishment and losses of old age; disappointment; grief over the loss of a spouse or child or parent, or close friend; unemployment; fighting to escape an addiction, or to remain sober; resisting the fear that makes people lie; standing by one's convictions in the face of opposition. The list of everyday heroisms is virtually endless. These ordinary men and women live with the silent, unsung conviction that God stands at the center of every human life. Perhaps without being able to explain how one does so, they know that they love God with all their heart, soul, mind, and strength; and in the selflessness with which they live from day to day, caring for their families and thinking about their neighbors, they demonstrate what it means to love others as one loves oneself. Such lives are without doubt signs of God's commitment to the world. They reveal the humble yet forceful way in which the Spirit, through all sorts of circumstances, constantly creates us by drawing us to life, provided, of course, we really want to be fully alive. Through the lives of believing men and women, the divine promise to stand by creation and lead it to the fullness of life becomes incarnate. Their lives sacramentalize for the whole Church the faithfulness of God to his people. They prove that the Spirit has never deserted the work of creation.

THE CHURCH AS KEEPER OF THE CREATION STORY

How then, we might ask, does the Church bear witness to divine faithfulness? First of all, the Church preserves the memory of the Creator's vision for the world, and for this alone we ought to be grateful. That there should be a permanent voice in human history reminding the world that it came from God, that the mystery of God is the secret of its deepest desires and identity, and that the fullness of life yet awaits it in God (and only in God): This is indeed a gift to the human race. For given the fact that we are social, historical creatures, how else could God have kept the divine promise before our minds and alive in our hearts, apart from a believing community that would continually remember and celebrate it in prayer and sacrament? We need reminders of our past lest we forget the most important truths about ourselves. And the Church, as witness to history, keeps our past in front of us. The community draws life from its faith about its origins, and because of that faith it envisions the future with hope. The God who presided over the act of creation will also preside over the ultimate liberation of all things from the power of death.

THE CHURCH: VOICE FOR JUSTICE

A second way in which the Church bears witness to divine faithfulness is through championing the great concerns of the prophets of old: justice, mercy, and forgiveness. God would not be a trustworthy advocate of the poor and oppressed unless, as he did through the prophets of old, God continued to condemn

70

every form of injustice. And this is exactly what the Church has done. Through its social teaching, the Church as an institution has provided a consistent message about economic justice, human dignity and rights, the evil of the arms race, and the destruction of powerless, voiceless men, women, and children in every part of the earth through hunger, illiteracy, poverty, and injustice. This has been especially true over the last hundred years, but the Church's social instinct goes back much farther to the days of the early Church writers—indeed, to the time of Jesus himself. One of the Church's functions, therefore, is to provide an abiding institutional witness to the biblical demand that men and women pursue the works of justice.

This institutional function has been matched by the personal witness of individual Christians. Frequently their actions have cost them their lives. They testify to the divine presence which has been accompanying the pilgrim people of God throughout the ages under the form of the crucified One. For when all is said and done, if the promise of God is fidelity to creation, then Jesus represents the divine promise in flesh and blood. The manner in which God chose to demonstrate that fidelity was to become a sojourner in history, joining men and women day by day amidst all the intricate details, moments, and events which make every human life both ordinary and interesting. If Jesus had not believed this and acted accordingly, then there would never have been a kingdom of God in his preaching; nor would there ever have been a community of followers — the Church — to take up where the Cross left off.

THE CHURCH AS BEARER OF THE MESSAGE OF FORGIVENESS

One of the recurring themes among the prophets was the kindness and mercy of God, a theme which figured prominently in the ministry of Jesus, too. No matter how faithless the people of Israel showed themselves, the promise of forgiveness was never revoked, provided, of course, that they changed their hearts: "Come now, let us set things right, says the Lord: Though your sins be like scarlet, they may become white as snow; though they be crimson red, they may become white as wool" (Isa 1:18). And again Scripture says,

"With age-old love I have loved you; so I have kept my mercy toward you. . . . [This] is the covenant which I will make with the house of Israel after those days, says the Lord. I will place my law within them, and write it upon their hearts; I will be their God, and they shall be my people. No longer will they have need to teach their friends and kinsmen how to know the Lord. All, from least to greatest, shall know me, says the Lord, for I will forgive their evildoing and remember their sin no more" (Jer 31:3, 33-34).

Forgiveness is so prominent among the prophets and in the work of Jesus that mercy, we can conclude, belongs to God's very essence, perhaps more than any other characteristic. The same love which led God to create the world leads God to redeem it, that is, to re-make it day by day, and no other trait so movingly and so forcefully reveals divine faithfulness to creation as mercy. God is a God of forgiveness because God is faithful; the full extent of that fidelity to a promise can only be gauged by the breadth of divine forgiveness: "Father, forgive them, they know not what they do" (Luke 23:34). It extends even to those who would murder God's Son. Forgiveness, we might say, is the principal way by which God continues to create human beings whose affections and orientation have been scarred by sin.

Although it is difficult to think of anything new to write about the theology of forgiveness, a lot can still be said about the experience of forgiveness, because there are so many forgiveness stories to be told. One afternoon, a young father with six children, was sitting on a bed in the family's cramped apartment. Only thirty-seven years old, and recently out of prison, he was dying. "I have the virus," he whispered. "I'm losing my hair, I can't gain any weight, I can't even climb stairs. Look at what's happened to me!" He then broke into heavy sobbing. When he had regained his composure, he said, "Do you know what the hardest thing of all is?" It was clear that he wanted to answer his own question. "It's being able to forgive yourself. How can you forgive anybody else, if you can't forgive yourself first?" This was something which, so far, he had not been able to do. As he listened to the kids shouting and playing in another room, he was once again conscious of the enormous guilt he felt about having to leave them. After all, he had been the one who had used the drugs; there was no one else to blame for his illness, whose onset had occurred six months before the birth of the youngest child. Two days before he died, he asked his ten-year-old daughter to take away his sins, "like the priest does."

Many of us have grown so accustomed to hearing about God's forgiveness and about the need to forgive one another, that it is sometimes easy to miss what the spiritual reality behind forgiveness is all about. Forgiveness is no doubt closely linked with guilt and sorrow; in fact, it presupposes some experience of them. Otherwise, the Church's teaching about the mystery of God's forgiveness falls on deaf ears. The fruit of forgiveness is reconciliation and peace: being one with God and with the neighbor whom we have offended. But basic to every other experience of reconciliation is the forgiving of oneself. The belief that God has forgiven us helps little if we have not been able to accept ourselves. Or maybe more precisely, the belief that God accepts us is the very thing which enables us to forgive and to accept our own sinful selves. This may explain why, in so many cases within the gospel, the restoration of the sinner is connected to being healed. It can be difficult to accept oneself if one's body is maimed or paralyzed or leprous or constantly oozing blood or subject to epileptic seizures. Yet physically disfigured people are not the only sinners in the world: All have sinned, and all stand in need of God's mercy. The ever-faithful God can do little for us, however, until we first become aware of what our personal sinfulness consists of.

The one who has sinned, and who truly knows his or her sins, has lived with sorrow and guilt: guilt over one's failures, over squandered talents and lost opportunities, over the betrayal of a friend's trust. Or the guilt might arise from having failed to meet another's need, from having dismissed someone's love, or from having spoiled another human life. It might come from having defrauded the poor or having taken delight in another's loss of innocence. One suddenly recognizes that, despite having succeeded admirably in the eyes of the world, one has failed miserably as a human being, provided that God out of mercy has kept alive in him some shred of conscience; material success may already have numbed her to the terrifying realization that he or she is the condemned rich man of the gospel story who never noticed the Lazarus outside his gate. Because of our guilt, we may feel that we have let down life itself, that precious gift which has been measured out to us and daily slips away. We come to realize that we have never really lived or never really responded to the gift of being on the earth. Such is the stuff of guilt. Is there any wonder, then, that God never proves himself more faithful to the divine promise than when he remains alongside of us as we come face to face with our sinfulness and guilt?

The Church, we have said, is a sign within history of the divine promise to be faithful to creation. The Church, as the community of Jesus' followers, stands alongside men and women, listening, counseling, encouraging, correcting, teaching, accepting, and, in God's name, forgiving. The Church which stays with us in our illness is not afraid to touch our infected bodies, anointing and blessing them as Jesus would have done. The Church which reassures the world of its Creator's love is not afraid to listen to the outpouring of human guilt and grief, and to help sinful human beings deal with their failures while assuring them of divine pardon and peace. Although it cannot undo human mistakes, the Church can help people re-orient their lives, lest they be trapped by the past. The Eucharistic mystery, above all, recalls and celebrates God's enduring promise to remain faithful to the world.

At the same time, it needs to be said that our openness to receiving divine forgiveness is contingent upon whether or not we have put on God's own attitude, for God forgives by blotting out our sins from the divine memory. God remembers our sins no more: "It is I, I, who wipe out, for my own sake, your offenses; your sins I remember no more" (Isa 43:25). Our relationship with God would be paralyzed if God continually remembered our sins. In the same way, human relationships cannot be repaired if one person is ready to offer forgiveness while the other person does not have the humility to accept it. The same holds true with an apology. One person's expression of sorrow is rendered useless if the other refuses to forget the offense. The properly Christian way to forgive, therefore, always presupposes that one possesses the attitude of God who forgives and "remembers no more" because God has compassion. And achieving compassion is the triumph of grace. The believing community, then, constantly has to challenge us to adopt the mind of Jesus. Jesus viewed the world contemplatively. He saw things as God does; he behaved as God would behave, which enables us to understand why he would say, "Be merciful, just as your Father is merciful" (Luke 6:36).

The promise to be faithful, as we have seen, implies the abiding offer of forgiveness, a promise which is first taught to us at baptism, recalled in sacramental reconciliation, and proclaimed in the mystery of bread and wine: "For this is my blood of the covenant, which will be shed on behalf of many for the forgiveness of sins" (Matt 26:28). It might even be said that the axis of all ministry in the Church is the mystery of reconciliation. Human beings, according to the biblical tradition, have been created for community; to be isolated, alienated, or marginalized is also to be incomplete as a man or as a woman. Since the beginning of its history, the Church has viewed the life and death of Jesus as bringing about reconciliation between God and the human race (although I think it makes better sense theologically to think of human beings needing to be reconciled to God, rather than God needing to be reconciled to the world; God, after all, never ran away from us). Paul writes: "And all this is from God, who has reconciled us to himself through Christ and given us the ministry of reconciliation, namely, God was reconciling the world to himself in Christ, not counting their trespasses against them and entrusting to us the message of reconciliation" (2 Cor 5:18-19).

The possibility of community, therefore, rests upon men and women being reconciled with one another, a possibility which will never be realized apart from their also being in union with God. For it is the Spirit of God that makes us desire to be together; it is the Spirit of God who raises up peacemakers and calls people to undertake the ministry of reconciliation. Without the Spirit in our hearts, true communion will never exist. Indeed, love itself does not exist apart from justice and faith. Concretely, this means that the Spirit of God constantly pushes the Church to be sensitive to whatever drives human beings apart: structures of economic injustice and political oppression; prejudice and racism; unequal access to the earth's resources; the unbridled ambition, greed, jealousy, and dishonesty which infect both interpersonal relationships and the relations between groups, social classes, and nations. Few people spontaneously and warmly welcome the prophetic voices that point to the barriers which keep people and nations apart. But only the most limited understanding of the nature of reconciliation would prevent us from admitting that such voices are truly of the Spirit.

Reconciling people with one another is often a dusty, tiring, and risky affair. One cannot bring peace and harmony to families without stepping into their homes, sharing in the complexities and anxieties of their lives. So too one should not expect to promote harmony and justice within societies without becoming enmeshed in their political, social, and economic problems. A great deal of the ferment caused in the last few years by the Church's addressing itself to issues such as economic exploitation, the arms race, the rights of the unborn and the death penalty, is truly a sign of the Spirit's presence within the Church. It is also a sign of God's carrying out the divine promise not to abandon the human race to moral or spiritual chaos.

Chapter Four

Spirit as Promise

If there was any single promise Jesus made to his followers, perhaps it was the pledge given at the moment of the Ascension:
"And behold, I am with you always, until the end of the age"
(Matt 28:20). In effect, Jesus had promised to remain among his
disciples until the close of human history. The glorification of
Jesus upon his Ascension to the Father's right hand did not mean
that he had withdrawn either from human history or from the
concerns of his disciples. The Ascension pledge merely recalled a
commitment he had made on an earlier occasion: "For where two
or three are gathered in my name, there I am in the midst of
them" (Matt 18:20). Whether we read these texts as formal
promises or as simple statements of fact, they firmly underscore
the early Church's belief in the abiding presence of Jesus. Indeed,
the abiding presence of Jesus at the heart of the community of his
disciples is the gift of the Spirit of God whom Jesus promised to
send, once he had been glorified: "But if I go, I will send [the
Advocate] to you" (John 16:7).

Not only does the Spirit reside in the community (which, as the
Spirit of God, is now the Spirit of Jesus as well); the Spirit also
dwells within each and every believer. The chief manifestation of
the Spirit's presence within us is love, and love is always of God.
As Paul writes, "[The] love of God has been poured out into our
hearts through the Holy Spirit that has been given to us" (Rom
5:5); and as John writes, "God is love, and whoever remains in
love remains in God and God in him" (1 John 4:16). The radiating
presence of love within the life of the community is the clearest
and surest evidence of God's promise to be faithful to creation,
for the wellspring of that love is the Spirit itself.

Not only is the abiding presence of Jesus within the community the Spirit's gift, but also it is actually *as* Spirit (as well as *through* the Spirit) that Jesus continues to dwell among his disciples. In and through the Spirit, Jesus, the living Lord, continues to teach and to guide his followers. He continues to instruct them about the mystery of the kingdom of God: about forgiveness and about justice, about faith and about hope, about who their neighbors are, about being poor and about being merciful, about what God is like and about how to live as God's daughters and sons. In short, Jesus continues to walk his followers along the way of the gospel. In all of this, the story of Jesus is truly the story of a promise kept. Jesus promised to remain with us, and one of the ways in which he does this is through the retelling of his story which, through image and memory, we can relive.

THE MAJOR WAYS IN WHICH JESUS REMAINS AMONG US

There are a number of customary ways in which the Church speaks about the abiding presence of Jesus: through sacraments, through Scripture, through the believing community as the Body of Christ, and through the individual believer as a temple of the Holy Spirit. The risen Jesus, according to the Church's traditional teaching, is truly present in each of the sacraments by means of sign, symbol, and ritual. Each sacrament in its own way deepens the relationship of the believer to the triune God, and it both renews and strengthens the inner life of the community. Each of the sacramental signs recalls a particular aspect of God's presence to us: a presence which is at once forgiving and healing, nourishing and strengthening, loving and empowering, sanctifying and divinizing. Precisely because they are symbolic expressions of the real presence of Jesus in the Church, the sacraments are multifaceted. They mean or signify many things. For underneath the Church's sacramental imagination lies the conviction that all created things point to the Creator as their source and thus are potentially revelatory of the holy mystery of God. Meal-taking and friendship, marriage and commitment, food and drink, family and community life, birth and death, sickness and diminishment: all of these human realities speak to us of our origins within the mystery of God. Ordinary activities such as washing and eating, embracing and the shaking of hands, love-making and giving birth, or everyday things such as water and light, oil and salt, or bread and wine, become the signs that trigger our imaginations to enter into a different world: a world that illuminates life, like a bright light shining from inside things, in order to reveal the truth about us and everything around us. For what is really real about us is that we come from God, that we are of God, and that we are for God, as the contemporary religious writer John S. Dunne puts it. Whenever human beings are in touch with this truth and live out of it, then the created world appears for what it is, namely, as sheer and utter gift.

The divine presence is not something imposed on our experience from outside, as if the mystery of God were foreign to the inner workings of our minds and hearts. That would merely reenforce the myth that the real world lies elsewhere and that the world of everyday life is but a mere shadow or type of something else. The classical distinction between the natural and the supernatural was intended to reaffirm the absolute graciousness of God, not to imply that God's love, goodness, and life were extrinsic to our humanity. Taking the existence of grace seriously, the sacramental imagination transforms our everyday experience and the ordinary realities which make it up so that, in effect, we learn to find God in all things. Needless to say, the notion of sacramentality embraces more than the traditional seven sacraments, for the Christian imagination is planted in the mystery of the Incarnation. The entire universe has to appear different to those who see in Jesus the Word of God made flesh, rooted by blood within our history and humanity; sharing our appetites, desires, and emotions; marveling and rejoicing at the marvelous things which God has made.

JESUS PRESENT IN THE STORY

Another important way in which the Spirit of Jesus abides within the community is through the constant retelling of the gospel story. The story of Jesus guides our imaginations, our prayer, and our actions. In fact, the symbolic action of the Church's sacramental rituals would be meaningless, apart from that story. Jesus' teaching and his parables, his encounters with people, his confrontations with political and religious authorities together with his prophetic denunciation of their abuse of power, his determination, his convictions about poverty and wealth, his faith in the extraordinary closeness of God, and his profound belief in both the reality and the imminence of the kingdom — these have become part and parcel of Christian religious sensibility. Impelled by the same Spirit which drove Jesus — a Spirit which it now shares — the community has internalized the attitudes of Jesus. It has put on the mind or attitude of Christ, as Paul would say (1 Cor 2:16; Phil 2:5). As a result, we have developed those habits of mind and heart which regularly interpret the world and experience through the eyes of the gospel.

The story of Jesus provides the categories and clues to which we appeal in order to decipher things and make sense of what we see and hear. How can we listen to stories about runaway children and great parental love without calling to mind the story of the prodigal son in Luke's gospel? How can we find ourselves in situations where we have been gravely offended, nursing hurt feelings and resentment, without recalling Jesus' saying about forgiveness, "I say to you, not seven times but seventy-seven times" (Matt 18:22)? And who does not listen to the words of the judgment scene in Matthew's gospel — "I was hungry and you gave me to eat, I was in prison and you visited me" — without undergoing an examination of conscience in order to determine whether his or her ability to see Jesus' face in such people has become dulled?

Jesus' parables about the kingdom often provide the imaginative keys out of which we describe what happens around us. The image of the mustard seed or of the lost sheep or of the distraught woman searching her house for a lost coin; the image of dough rising or of a forgotten treasure buried in a field or of a man assaulted by robbers while journeying from Jerusalem to Jericho; the picture of a poor widow conned by religious figures "who devour the houses of widows" (Mark 12:40) into believing that God would be pleased if she donated all she had to live on to an institution which was about to come tumbling down; the scene of the unemployed laborers lingering around the town square waiting for someone to hire them; the image of the foolish virgins who al-

lowed their lamps to run out of oil; or the scene of a prophet undone by the hatred of a queen and the cowardice of her husband;
these and many other gospel images and memories have entered
into the way the Christian reads and thinks about reality. And
central to all of these scenes is the familiar image of the Cross itself, an image which has become a symbol of the intersection of
suffering and love, a sign which calls people to put on the mind
and heart of Jesus — indeed, an image which represents the great
mystery of God's unconquerable love for the human race. Images
and scenes such as these provide the basic materials out of which
the Christian imagination constructs its universe or world of
meaning.

What happens to us through the images, scenes and encounters
of the gospel narratives is that we gradually learn to view our experience in gospel terms. People and events assume gospel
proportions. Tortured faces of the world's poor staring out at us
from our newspapers and television sets bring to mind the story,
"There was a rich man who dressed in purple garments and fine
linen and dined sumptuously each day. And lying at his door was
a poor man named Lazarus. . . ." (Luke 16:19-20) Accounts of
people forced to survive on the streets make us think of the question, "When did we see you a stranger and welcome you, or
naked and clothe you?" (Matt 25:38) Situations of enormous ten-
sion or anxiety may cause us to recall the episode of Jesus' calm-
ing the wind and the waves for his frightened disciples. For many
people, the activity of meal-taking is colored by the memory of
Jesus having been found so often at table with all sorts of people:
taking meals together is humanly all the richer because, for Jesus,
fellowship at table expressed the nearness and acceptance of God.
Massive food production and distribution, especially against the
background of global poverty and hunger, might be viewed by
Christians as a contemporary expression of the multiplication of
loaves and fishes, while our experience of humble beginnings and
uncelebrated results recalls the parable of the mustard seed.

Discussion about unemployment and the need to obtain basic
material goods with dignity can draw us to remember the un-
settling story about the vineyard owner who paid each of his
laborers according to their need, not according to the amount of

time they worked, for the parable was a story about *God's* understanding of justice, not man's. Reports of political corruption, injustice, and the abuse of power confirm that the Herods and Pilates of this world still thrive, while the scribes and Pharisees often discover their contemporary counterparts in the arrogance and hypocrisy of economic, political, and religious establishments. Tax-collectors and prostitutes — the gospel's professional sinners — can be found among the outcasts and publicly marginalized people of our day: homosexuals and drug-addicts, ex-prisoners and the illiterate unemployed. Gospel scenes and stories are like transparencies spread over everything. For those who want to live the kingdom, as Jesus did, these transparencies transform the reality around us so that we, too, start to think, to imagine, and to act in much the same way that Jesus did.

The world of everyday life, however, with all its ordinary events, people, and circumstances, as well as with all its larger moments in the political and social world of which we are a part: this real world, which seems so eminently sturdy and dependable, appears to throw the world of the gospel into unreality. For it might be objected, Jesus lived at a very different time and place. Not only that, Jesus could afford to read the world God's way and to make God the center of everything; he, after all, was God's Son. Today, one enters Jesus' world only through the historically unreliable power of imagination, a power which all too easily romanticizes a past which the religious heart understandably yet mistakenly endeavors to recapture and to love. We, however, living in a more sophisticated age, can excuse ourselves from taking the kingdom of God as seriously as Jesus did. Our present existence is the only one we know. Compared to it, anything else must seem like a fantasy world: interesting, even attractive, but imaginary nonetheless. How, then, can we be blamed if we take the present state of things to be their real state and reject the world of the gospel as fanciful and unstable, however inspired and pious it might sometimes make us feel? We cannot afford to jeopardize our lives for a hope which failed to materialize. We may try to imitate Jesus' attitudes and faith up to a point, but after that the principle of realism takes over.

But the gospel story does not let us off the hook so smoothly. If no other parable or miracle, no other teaching or encounter wakes up our souls, then at least the Cross — the crucified Jesus — will keep probing us concerning what, ultimately, we would risk our lives for. Maybe only by means of this question, spoken from the Cross, will we finally come to face the truth: Will our souls be shallow or deep, hollow or full of grace? Will we be vigorously compassionate men and women, people who steadfastly refuse to trade their integrity for anything, or will we be men and women who notice nothing but themselves, people who have let their souls be dazzled and tricked by those with the illusory power to turn stones into bread or pennies into fortunes? The Cross may be about sacrifice of life, but it is not about loss of soul: "What profit is there for one to gain the whole world yet lose or forfeit himself?" (Luke 9:25) Such is the question which falls from the lips of the crucified Jesus.

To repeat, the Gospels disclose a different world, a different way of existing. They invite us to imagine the possibility of a humanity enhanced and enriched by that liberating faith which is engendered by the Spirit of God. The Gospels rearrange our categories of what is important and what is not, what is worth living (and dying) for and what is not. The Gospels place before us an entirely different set of priorities and values from what our culture prizes. Yet, paradoxically, it is only from within the world of the gospel that one truly understands what everyday reality consists of, for the Gospels expose the unreality and deception which invade everyday life both within our families and neighborhoods, as well as within the wider world of cities, nations, and states with all their economic, social, and political institutions.

The Gospel represents the "word of the Lord," a word addressed to our age just as surely as the words spoken by the prophets of old were addressed to the men and women of their day. That word cuts into our world and across our lives, slicing away their shallowness and exposing the flight from reality which infects our time and place in history. Though written some two thousand years ago, the Gospels — even with their images and scenes drawn from a different culture and epoch — continue to bring us the word of the Lord. Through that word, the Spirit of Jesus turns our world upside down in the same way that Jesus upset the world of his audience, challenging the men and women of his day to change their hearts and mend their ways because the kingdom — the reality — of God was at hand. What else would we expect the abiding presence of Jesus to mean? Jesus' promise to remain among his followers at least has to include this: that in and through the Spirit, Jesus, as the living Lord, continues to do in our day what he did in his own time, namely, to call people to lead their lives out of faith, to live in the truth, to accept the kingdom, and to discover for themselves the reality of God's presence among them. That is, they must lay aside sin, recognize their self-deception and flight from the truth, renounce the counter-kingdom of Satan and their enslavement to its charms, and refuse anything which would preempt their freedom as children of God. In telling the story of Jesus, the Church renders Jesus truly present. In listening to that story, we run the risk of making it our story, too. We could genuinely become the disciples.

Over the course of the twentieth century, there have been many attempts to recover the history of Jesus. Aware that the evangelists composed their narratives from the perspective of Easter faith, biblical scholars have tried to locate the story beneath the story. In large part, this scholarly effort has been prompted by the peculiar sensitivity of men and women today to history and historical fact. We do not want to base our faith on something which is only a story, however beautiful and inspiring it may be. If the gospels are merely stories, loosely weaving together history and faith, how can we be sure that what we are believing is correct and truly worth trusting?

The fact is that all of us are believers because we have been brought into contact with others who are believers, too. The Christian faith has been socially transmitted over the centuries since the very beginning when the frightened women ran from the empty tomb of Jesus with the astonishing news that he had been raised from the dead. Faith, in other words, builds upon faith, generation after generation. No one has some sort of primary, privileged access to the events behind the Church's belief.

But the real aim of the biblical scholarship which has been searching for the historical Jesus, or at least the real Catholic aim, is not history so much as faith. To be sure, the result of so much research, study, and scholarship has been that we now know a lot more about the history of Jesus, the composition of the gospels, and the New Testament times than was ever known before. And a second result is that we have a much firmer grasp of the humanness of Jesus than the generations before us, whose understanding of Jesus tended to be strongly weighted on the side of divinity. But the major result has been that we have been able to view, again perhaps more clearly than ever before, the faith of Jesus.

Faith builds upon faith, as we have already noted. The disciples' faith was founded upon the faith *of* Jesus long before the Church came to speak about faith *in* Jesus. Or to put the matter a little differently, it was the disciples' exposure to the faith *of* Jesus which ultimately led them to place their faith *in* Jesus. What historical research has brought us to, therefore, is faith: more precisely, to Jesus' faith. At its core, this is what the gospel story is all about. The disciples believed, and we believe, because *Jesus* was a believer. And perhaps the key element of his faith, the piece which must have ignited the deepest human desires and longings of the disciples, was that it was so liberating: faith sets human beings free to live for others, as mature sons and daughters of God. Even today, the power of the story proves itself, for within that narrative human beings continue to encounter the liberating presence of God.

JESUS PRESENT WITHIN US

There is a variation on the divine promise which can be derived from the Fourth Gospel. As we have explained in previous chapters, essentially there is but one promise, namely, God's promise to be faithful to creation. Whatever other promises a person may find in Scripture are variations upon that one, initial promise. In John's Gospel, Jesus speaks to us, it often sounds, from the other side of glory as one who has been definitively united with God. From its experience of the risen Jesus dwelling in its midst, John's community heard Jesus say things such as, "Whoever eats this bread will live forever" (John 6:51), "Whoever believes in me, as scripture says: 'rivers of living water will flow from within him' "

(John 7:38), and "Whoever follows me will not walk in darkness, but will have the light of life" (John 8:12). In each of these instances, Jesus has promised eternal life, the very life of God, which is best characterized as love itself. As such, that life has already begun, for those who have placed their faith in Jesus, the one whom the Father has sent (John 5:37).

Eternal life is Jesus' great promise in the Gospel of John. This is the life intended for us from the very beginning by the Creator, who has been revealed to us as the Father of Jesus, the community's risen Lord. What that life concretely means for us here and now is spelled out in a multiplicity of ways in the other three Gospels. It means being mindful of those who are poor or imprisoned or sick or strangers in our midst; it means forgiveness and compassion, as the Father himself is compassionate; it means honesty and integrity, and resisting whatever oppresses other men and women, who are truly one's sisters and brothers. In the Fourth Gospel, all of this can be reduced to love and service, in imitation of the one who has been among us as one who serves: "I have given you a model to follow, so that as I have done for you, you should also do" (John 13:15), and "I give you a new commandment: love one another. As I have loved you, so you also should love one another. This is how all will know that you are my disciples" (John 13:34-35).

Eternal life within us arises from our union with Jesus in the Spirit. He had said, "The Father and I are one" (John 10:30) and again, speaking to his disciples, "Remain in me, as I remain in you" (John 15:4). Just as Jesus was one with the Father and this union with the Father was what gave Jesus his unique status as the Son, so too the individual believer becomes one with Jesus. This union with his Spirit makes us share in the holy mystery of God in a singular way. The same Spirit which made Jesus who he was, which empowered him, which made possible his experience of God and enabled him to trust it, that very Spirit has been given to us. The Spirit thus makes us who we are, too. It empowers us. It enables us to experience God as Jesus knew God by making it possible for us to be-with-Jesus. Being-with-Jesus is to know and to experience God in a brand new way. The Spirit itself liberates us to let go of everything and to answer the God whom

Jesus knew, about whom he spoke, and whose kingdom he believed in.

John's Gospel tells us that Jesus did what he did, and said what he said, because he first learned from the Father: "Amen, Amen, I say to you, a son cannot do anything on his own, but only what he sees his father doing; for what he does, his son will do also. For the Father loves the Son and shows him everything that he himself does" (John 5:19-20). The son speaks nothing of himself. He says only what he has heard from the Father: "[What] I heard from him I tell the world. . . . I do nothing on my own, but I say only what the Father taught me" (John 8:26, 28). Because of his union with the Father, the works Jesus did were truly the works of God; it was the Father who worked through him.

The disciples of Jesus could make a similar claim. The disciples do nothing on their own; they do only what they have first "seen" Jesus doing. Nor do they speak anything on their own. They speak only what they have first "heard" Jesus saying. And because of their union with the Spirit of Jesus, it might truly be said that whenever the disciples act, it is actually Jesus speaking and acting through them. Again, Jesus had said to his disciples, "Do you not believe that I am in the Father and the Father is in me? The words I speak to you I do not speak on my own. The Father who dwells in me is doing his works" (John 14:10). He had become their living bread (John 6:48), the light of their life (8:12), the one who satisfied their soul's deepest thirst (7:37). In short, they were drawing life from him. Might the disciples of Jesus not rephrase his statement, therefore, and say something like this to those who would question them: "Do you not believe that we are in Jesus and that Jesus is in us? The words we speak are not our own, and the things we do are not proceeding from us, but from the Spirit of Jesus who dwells within us."

It is important that we take time to meditate upon the profound mystery which each of us is, or can become, by being a Christian. Our union with the Spirit of Jesus, a union which totally transforms our humanity, has to be presupposed before we can ever set about transforming and renewing the earth. Yes, it is we who must engage in the hundreds of things which concretely will bring about that change; but, no, it is not finally our work that brings about the kingdom of God. Yes, we are co-workers with God in the ongoing labor of creation; but, no, we are not the creators of the world which God intends to bring about. The redemption, transformation, and full liberation of humanity is nothing less than the human being fully united with the Spirit, just as Jesus was completely one with the Father, who is now our Father, too (John 20:17). In all of this, God is making good on the divine promise: God fulfills the promise to remain faithful to the world by being faithful to it through men and women like us.

The Christian life — indeed, the Christian person himself or herself — is totally unintelligible apart from this profound truth which the Fourth Gospel has been teaching us. Occasionally, one hears simplistic formulations about what the gospels are calling us to. For some, being Christian means activity; for others, it means contemplation. For some, it means promoting social and political change in order to usher in the kingdom of God. For others, it means inner directedness, personal moral renewal, prayer, and pursuing a private relationship with God. It may be equally simplistic to conclude that being Christian involves both elements: action and contemplation; engagement with the world, and interior union with the silent mystery of God. The solution involves a little more than the facile combination of two important elements, namely, prayer and praxis. It also involves a thoroughgoing immersion in the story of Jesus and a prolonged exposure to his faith.

For Jesus, prayer was not simply the animating force behind his action, although this is a common way of conceiving the role of prayer in human life. Nor was he just an intensely active prophet whose inner compass was constantly centered on God, as if action and contemplation were like two intersecting lines, with one line stretching horizontally across the earth and the other pointing vertically toward heaven. Jesus' union with the Father was much more subtle and pervasive than this approach to spirituality might suggest, because his notion of God was thoroughly integrated into everyday life. Consequently, for Jesus, religion would never be fundamentally a matter of introspective meditation since God could never be adequately pictured merely as a silent, inner light, the all-holy mystery ever to be prayed to, adored, and loved. In other words, there was no other-worldly mysticism in Jesus' faith. The God of Jesus was mysteriously and profoundly close to this world and passionately aware of its concerns, and his God certainly could not be relegated to being the preoccupation or preserve of professional holy people.

Consider the miracles of Jesus. They were not proofs of his possessing divine status or even mere confirmations of his teaching. The miracles drew attention to the nearness of the kingdom; one could even read them as protests against the way things were. The miracles of Jesus were saying, in effect, that God did not want people to be blind or lame or deaf; God did not decree poverty or social marginalization, leprosy, or paralysis. The God of Jesus did not want parents to see their children dying before their eyes, or to watch human beings tormented by demons, or even to have a young couple's wedding party spoiled by wine running out. The God whose Spirit enabled Jesus to perform such actions was not a God whose presence or whose heart was distant from us, or whose concerns were purely spiritual. This was the God who had listened to the cries of the poor, who has joined the anguished protests of all men and women who are struggling to live with decency and in freedom. The God of Jesus desired human wholeness. And because Jesus was a believer, the miracles — the protests before God — were possible, for "Everything is possible to one who has faith" (Mark 9:23).

We need, therefore, to be cautious in the way we conceive the relationship between action and contemplation. Without intending to, we could do a disservice to the story of Jesus and fail to comprehend what sort of God it is who creates the world, invests in it passionately (as the prophets have demonstrated), and continually prompts men and women to struggle on behalf of justice. The Christian contemplation of God, the Christian experience of God arises from within the world, not from the heavens. "Men of Galilee," said the messenger on the day of the Ascension, "why are you standing there looking at the sky?" (Acts 1:11)

WHEN PROJECTS FAIL

Jesus, we have already remarked, shared the apocalyptic mentality of his time which anticipated that God's definitive action in history, the inauguration of the messianic era, was just around the corner. On this point, both Jesus and his contemporaries were mistaken. One can readily understand, however, how an individual who is charismatically fired for mission would be thinking and acting within a very special mind-set. Even apart from the apocalypticism which was prevalent in his day, Jesus' own enthusiasm, his sense of the nearness of God, and, therefore, of the imminence of the kingdom would have led him to regard the many human needs of men and women with a striking sense of urgency.

The charismatic, grace-filled prophet who sees the needs of his people is going to feel the immediacy of God in the sharpest possible way. For the fact of the matter was that Jesus had experienced God's call, profoundly and dramatically, when he was baptized by John. To have felt himself called and to have heard God claiming, "You are my beloved Son; with you I am well pleased" (Mark 1:11), must have led him to view his life and mission in terms of the utmost intensity. The weeks and months which followed would have been marked by a passionate determination to complete the work of John the Baptist, the imprisoned prophet, and announce the kingdom of God. Life, for Jesus, would have assumed a sense of ultimacy and finality.

As we have already seen, the fact that Jesus, like so many others, was wrong about the timing of the kingdom's arrival, should not be so disturbing as it sounds. In fact, Jesus might even have been mistaken about how, exactly, God actually was working within history, although the kingdom parables in the thirteenth chapter of Matthew's Gospel suggest that, at least for Matthew, Jesus seems to have envisioned the final harvest in terms of the long haul of history. Actually, it does not really matter. What did not happen then, all at once, has been slowly taking place down through the centuries. Hope for the restoration of Israel had to give way to hope for the gradual transformation and liberation of the other nations and peoples of the world because God had created them, too. The community of Jesus, then, still announces, still hopes and remains vigilant, and still continues the ministry of Jesus.

In Jesus' case, the failure was neither a matter of timing nor the manner of conceiving the kingdom. Rather, the failure consisted of the lack of response on the part of men and women to the call for change of heart, repentance, and conversion. The disappointment which Jesus must surely have felt, which finally issued in his desperate cry from the Cross points to a keen sense of having been let down, even betrayed, by God: "My God, my God, why have you forsaken me?" (Mark 15:34). After all, God had sought out Jesus. God had intervened in his life and chosen him, driven him into the wilderness, and poured the Spirit into his heart, his words and his hands. Having done all that, how, Jesus might have wondered, could God have brought him to such a pass? If God had foreseen that people would not accept Jesus' summons to conversion, then why had God bothered in the first place? Or might Jesus have sadly recalled his own parable about how a trusting landowner, betrayed by a bloodthirsty band of thieves to whom he had rented his property, continued to send servants and messengers, and even, finally, his own son. "What then," Jesus had asked, "will the owner of the vineyard do?" (Mark 12:9). Indeed, what more could he do to make the tenants listen to reason?

The parable goes on to say that the vineyard owner will come and put them to death, and under the circumstances we can understand why the story would conclude on the note of punishment and thereby satisfy our sense of justice. But as the New Testament scholar John R. Donahue points out, it is equally plausible that Jesus could have left his audience with that question dangling in their ears, "What then will the owner of the vineyard do?" And a possible answer would be that the owner would have to come in person and try to persuade his tenants to honor their agreement. In short, the sense of the story is that God apparently never gives up, in spite of persistent rejection and hardness of heart. Such an open ending, of course, is exactly how the Christian story goes: the "son" was killed, and "thrown" (or buried) outside the "vineyard" (or outside the holy city). But what followed was not avenging legions of angels, but resurrection and the preaching of the message all over again, this time by the disciples. God, in effect, had not yet given up on calling men and women to repentance and change of heart.

Perhaps the outcome of Jesus' life did not conform to his enthusiastic expectations, but it was hardly a failure. And this fact, this great mystery, always stands behind the Cross. The Christian does not behold the crucified Jesus without somehow sensing the truth of Paul's insight, "We know that all things work for good for those who love God" (Rom 8:28). God never loses in projects initiated by the Spirit of life.

The experience of failure, coupled with the hope that God somehow brings good out of every holy endeavor, is an essential characteristic of the Christian story. Countless parents, having related in their own manner to the story of Jesus, know what this means. For sometimes, despite their sincerest efforts, prayer, patience, and love, a son or daughter turns out painfully contrary to their hopes and dreams. People make plans which never materialize, projects collapse, and even a vision which has arisen in the Spirit can fail to take root. In fact, those who should understand best the ways of the Spirit are frequently the very ones who bring down what God has inspired! Again, the parables of Jesus may shed light on this experience. We can imagine Jesus, too, wondering why men and women had failed to respond to his preaching as vigorously as he had hoped. Maybe he was thinking about that while sitting on a stone wall somewhere in a field in Galilee, distractedly watching a farmer sow his seed. Then, all at once, things would have "clicked." The image of the farmer, trailed by some birds pecking at the seed which fell upon the path, or upon the rocks, clarified his experience of sowing God's prophetic words. Sometimes, things do not grow because they fail to reach the proper soil. Yet in the long run, the sower wins: the harvest, the final yield, can defy our most extravagant expectations. In the long run, God does not lose. In the long run, nothing sown in love, nothing endeavored in response to the Spirit, can fail. This belongs to the Spirit's promise.

Loving God in the Dark

A promise, we remarked in the Introduction, is the way by which human beings love in the dark. Through our promises, we entrust ourselves to one another, committing ourselves to our word even though the future is largely hidden from our eyes. By means of the making and accepting of promises, we build lifegiving security into reality. On this basis, we learn to trust the world; on the basis of this trust, relationships are created, families are brought into being, and communities form and thrive. The fact is that human beings can and do make lifelong promises. While it is undoubtedly true that circumstances can arise which make it very difficult, even sometimes impossible, to keep a promise, it is also true that men and women do, with God's help, frequently surmount the severest challenges and remain true to their word. They achieve this everyday heroism, not by sheer force of will or by mindless resignation to conditions and events they feel to be outside their control, but by love. Love makes sacrifice and the keeping of promises possible. That is why those who struggle to keep their promises become ever more fully human. Promises, openly and honestly given, do not limit our freedom; they enhance it, and thereby they also enhance one's humanity.

Not only do we make promises to one another, however. We also make promises to God. But these are of a different nature from our other promises. In the promises we make and receive from one another, we normally promise to do something. The marriage promise is a special kind because two friends who marry promise mutual love and fidelity, not just for a specified period of time, but for the rest of their lives. That is the Christian ideal, mirroring, as it does, the Creator's everlasting love and fidelity toward the human race as well as toward each and every one of us.

The promises we make to God, on the other hand, are actually less promises to *do* something than to *be* something. Indeed, it could be argued (as we did) that all of our promises are ultimately spoken to God since behind every promise there stands the pledge to be, in the Creator's sight, a man or woman of truth. But the promises we make explicitly to God (for example, at baptism) translate the heart's desire to be a man or a woman of faith, hope, and love. They express the soul's longing actually to be a daughter or son of God, a beloved child with whom the Father will be as well pleased as he was with Jesus. Promises to God, in other words, reveal the human soul's most earnest desire and prayer.

But promises have to be freely accepted as well as freely and maturely given. God, then, has to accept our promises because it was God who implanted the desire for love and for life within us in the first place. And because God gave the desire, God also provides the possibility for fulfilling our promises, which is called grace. In this way, the divine promise to creation is being kept: "The Lord is faithful in all his words and holy in all his works" (Ps 145:13). Perhaps the main way in which we sense the ongoing fidelity of God to us, that is, the divine acceptance of our heart's desire and promise, is love. One experiences oneself loved, brought into existence, brought into this world, because one has been loved: loved by parents, yes; loved by family and friends, yes. But more truly and more profoundly, the love that brought us to life came from God. First and foremost, we are children of God, "born not by natural generation nor by human choice nor by a man's decision but of God" (John 1:13). Such is the guiding sense of divine faithfulness. That sense accompanies us even through our darkest hours, as it did Jesus. At the end, Jesus may have felt abandoned by God (Mark 15:34). But it was not an abandonment unaccompanied by faith, for he could also add, "Father, into your hands I commend my spirit" (Luke 23:46). Jesus, we might say, had learned how to love God in the dark.

If that is how things stood with Jesus, who is God's child in an eminent and unique way, then what might the rest of us expect? Just as the keeping of the promises we make to one another often demands loving in the dark, so too does the keeping of the promises we make to God. We continue to love and remain loyal to the holy mystery of God, who is the silent, holy mystery of our lives, even when life appears to be presenting us with every reason not to believe. There are occasions when one is tempted to renounce one's faith and in one's bitterness to disavow that guiding sense of having been born, not by natural generation or human choice but of God. One may be tempted to despair; one may even allow that temptation to cross one's lips. But it crosses in words which embody, when all is said and done, a prayer: for to whom else would one direct one's protest, one's bitterness and one's feeling of abandonment, except to the One who is able to save us from death and who hears us because of our reverence (cf. Hebrews 5:7)? Bitterness — together with the feelings of anger, of being disillusioned, and abandoned — does not have to cancel out faith, nor does it have to cancel out love. Whether measured in terms of moments or years (time does not seem to matter when the soul is learning what God is like), the heart learns how to listen to God, how to be reverent, through the things that it suffers. It learns that there is no life in anything except love, even when everything around us appears to be contradicting this one great law.

What helps me to understand experiences such as these is the realization that God must be suffering with us through the darkness that invades our lives, just as human parents suffer with their children in their pain and grief no matter how grown the children are or no matter whether the pain results from bad fortune, honest mistakes, or their children's own foolishness. God by no means watches human history passively, certainly not if the story of Jesus has any relevance. In fact, since the Creator's love remains steadily faithful throughout the history of the human race, we might even say that the history of the human race is the story of God's promise. At the same time, that history is a story about God's loving us in the dark: but in *our* darkness, in the agonizing night of our wrestling with demons (as Jesus did in Gethsemane), not in God's darkness. We cannot see in the dark or into the unseen future, so out of our love we make promises. God, however, sees ahead, as it were. Thus the reason for the divine promise has to be for our sake. In the biblical story, God makes a promise in order to reassure us of lasting fidelity throughout a future which we cannot grasp. In this way, then, the promise of God becomes our future. Or to put the idea more simply still, God and the promise of God are one.

HOPE ON TRIAL

In the Acts of the Apostles, Luke reports a scene where Paul found himself facing a certain King Agrippa and the Roman governor Porcius Festus. Concluding his defense, Paul said: "But now I am standing trial because of my hope in the promise made by God to our ancestors. . . . Why is it thought unbelievable among you that God raises the dead?" (Acts 26:6, 8). The promise of God, Paul implies, is nothing less than the raising of the dead to life. To be sure, Paul specifically has the resurrection of Jesus in mind. Yet there is the broader truth which the raising of Jesus has confirmed, namely, that the destiny of the human being is a definitive, irreversible union with God: the "ascension" of each and every one of us into glory. The power of the Father's love, so forcefully revealed in the raising of Jesus from the dead, continues to work in history in order to bring about the redemption, the full creation of the human race. In short, God and the promise are one.

It must be said, though, that the significance of the resurrection bears on this life and not primarily on the next. The fact is that Jesus' being raised from the dead carried implications. The resurrection implied that God in Jesus was more intimately immersed in ordinary human life than anyone might have suspected. Paul had been arrested and was put on trial because of his bearing witness to the divine promise. But why was the resurrection such a dangerous belief? What was so threatening about hope in the resurrection of the dead? True, there was a debate between the Sadducees and the Pharisees as to whether there actually would be a resurrection (Luke 20:27), and this is reflected in the controversy reported in the Acts of the Apostles (23:6, 24:21). Yet the Pharisees, who likewise believed in the resurrection of the dead, had not been arrested. The reason has to be that Paul had been proclaiming the raising of *Jesus* from the dead; the general religious hope had suddenly become concrete in the story of Jesus. And if the Father had raised Jesus, then something was being revealed about the importance and the identity of the teacher from Nazareth. God had vindicated Jesus' mission; God had endorsed Jesus' life and teaching.

The episode of Paul's arrest and trial indicates both the danger of believing in God's promise ("I am standing trial because of my hope in the promise made by God to our ancestors") as well as the risk involved in testifying to the risen Jesus ("Why is it thought unbelievable among you that God raises the dead?"). If Jesus has been raised, then the consequence must be repentance, so as to obtain divine forgiveness (Acts 26:20). Those most threatened by Paul's preaching of the raising of Jesus would have been those people most challenged by the preaching of Jesus, too. Paul's hope in the divine promise had radicalized him; he could face any opposition, speak boldly, and even gladly welcome the sufferings his mission caused him because the same had happened to Jesus.

Obviously, it would be incorrect to conclude that Christianity offered the possibility of the forgiveness of sins, and that this was what distinguished it from Judaism. For the point was not that the gospel stood for forgiveness, or even that forgiveness was being offered too readily. Rather, the difficulty was that the road to forgiveness had to be paved through conversion or change of heart. What gets the apostle or the prophet into trouble is the business of identifying those things which need to be acknowledged as evil, the sins from which individuals and groups need to repent. It is one thing to proclaim "Repent"; it is quite another thing to say, "It is not lawful for you to have your brother's wife" (Mark 6:18).

To some degree, the disciple of Jesus will always be on trial before the nonbelieving world for his or her hope. That is why the First Letter of Peter could urge, "Always be ready to give an explanation to anyone who asks you for a reason for your hope" (3:15). But the greater reason for being brought to trial is what our hope leads us to do. For our hope is joined to the divine promise, and the divine promise is not only resurrection but liberation. Freedom from the power of death, precisely as God's action, begins in this world with the liberation of human beings from all that oppresses them. The God who delivers slaves from bondage has not undergone a personality change; the divine saving action has not become more "spiritual" as opposed to this-worldly and historical as a result of the resurrection of Jesus. After all, the resurrection of Jesus can mean only as much as the story which precedes it. Isolated from that story, Jesus' resurrection amounts to little more than a personal affirmation, a reward to him for his obedience which has little reference to us here and now.

Thus according to that story, Jesus (and his mother, too) believed in a God who tore down the mighty from their thrones and lifted up the lowly, who filled the hungry with good things and sent the rich away empty (Luke 1:51-53). This conviction borders on revolution. It is good news to the poor, but it is bad news for anyone who has a vested interest in keeping the world or society the way it is. Perhaps that explains why believing that God raised Jesus of Nazareth from the dead was, and remains today, so dangerous.